How to Graduate from College the Easy Way ... and Other Popular Fairy Tales

Why college success in the real world is about hard work and knowing yourself.

A practical, real-life, totally new approach to living happily ever after.

By Sidney Pogatchnik and Mark Kroh
Illustrations by Nina Finn-Kelcey

CampusToolKit™
Navigator Edition

Campus ToolKit – York, Pennsylvania

How to Graduate from College the Easy Way ... and Other Popular Fairy Tales

Published by Campus ToolKit
303 East Market Street
York, Pennsylvania 17403
877.303.3023
www.campustoolkit.com

ISBN: 978-0-9795098-0-3

Library of Congress Catalog Card Number: 2007929054

Printed in the United States of America.

Publisher's Acknowledgements
We're proud of this book. Please register your comments online at
http://www.campustoolkit.com/comments

Layout, cover design, graphics and other designs: Larry Daughenbaugh
Proofreaders: Heather Tull, Kari Kroh and Larry Daughenbaugh

Printed on recycled paper.

"Do not let your fire go out, spark by irreplaceable spark. In the hopeless swamps of the not quite, the not yet, and the not at all, do not let the hero in your soul perish and leave only frustration for the life you deserved, but have never been able to reach. The world you desire can be won, it exists, it is real, it is possible, it is yours."

– Ayn Rand, Atlas Shrugged

~ Contents ~

CONTENTS

~ Overview ~
The Keys to the Kingdom

Let's start with the title of this book – How to Graduate from College the Easy Way … and Other Popular Fairy Tales. What do we mean *"other popular fairy tales?"* Basically, we are talking about the fact that a lot of books you see for first year college students want to make it seem like all you have to do is learn some simple tricks and you'll breeze through to that degree. And, well, there ARE some simple tricks that will make your academic life easier. But here's the thing. Tricks aren't the answer. They just aren't enough to carry you through to the end. College is an incredible time of change and growth and that's hard stuff. Students need to have strength, motivation, support, goals and the knowledge of how to make all these things work together. Then, they need to practice these skills until they are second nature. That's why we've written this book and created the companion web site, Campus ToolKit.

Campus ToolKit is your own personal kit full of tools to help you succeed in college (so it's not just a clever name.) In fact, there is so much information that it wouldn't all fit into this book . For example, there are ten whole chapters on improving your study skills that are only available online. Amazing. As for this book, the most amazing part of this it is you. Because this book is based on you, personally.

Now, how can we do that? It's a book, after all. So how can we know about you, personally? Well, this brings us back to that tool kit and the tools contained therein. Since there is only one **you** in this world, our job is to help you learn all about who you are, what makes you tick, and how you can make the most of your unique set of skills and talents.

The idea behind this book came when we were writing our online knowledge modules for students (more on those later). We realized that there wasn't just *one solution* for success in college because, hey! We're all different. There isn't just *one* solution to procrastination, or time management, or more effective studying, or meeting new people. What works for your older brother or your next-door neighbor might not work for you at all. Likewise, if you're a super-successful student, you could explain your methods until you're blue in the face but it doesn't mean they will work for anyone else. Because people are different.

This isn't just a book about study methods, either, because college isn't just about studying! Don't get us wrong; getting the best grades possible is job number one in college. Good grades and staying on top of studies make up your foundation in college. Without that strong foundation, everything else tends to go downhill in a hurry, including your social life. However, whether you're attending straight from high school or are a returning student of any age, you'll probably make interesting new friends in college. College is an opportunity to meet other people and learn about yourself in the process.

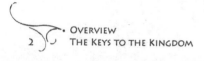

Money is another biggie. For most people, having enough money in college is a perpetual struggle. If you're a returning student, you might have had to cut back on hours at work to accommodate your new course schedule. If you're a student in your first year or so out of high school, you'll most likely be as broke as can be - it's just the way things are. If you're fortunate enough to be… well, *not* broke during college, this system will give you valuable information about how to make your money go further, and how to start growing a financial empire now. At the very least you will gain an insightful understanding of the plight of those around you. It isn't personal. They really *can't afford to* go to the movies Saturday night!

So what is Campus ToolKit? Well, as soon as we realized that people were different, and that one solution wasn't going to work for everybody, we began the search for tools that would help you understand exactly who you are, and what your distinct personality type is. We knew that when we found the right ones, we could give you a tool kit without limits. We want to give you a mirror into your own mind, and helpful suggestions to get through college in the easiest way possible… *your way*!

So what's in this thing?

Campus ToolKit is a personalized system made of two components: this book, and online information and tools. The book contains practical information for college success, and leads you through all of the online tools. Your online space is where you will discover information about yourself by taking special assessments and quizzes. Your Campus ToolKit online system is also full of practical features to help you every day in college.

Everything in Campus Toolkit is designed to help you cope, and come out ahead in college. Upon entering the online system with the enrollment key found at the back of this book, you'll see a very simple page with shortcuts to tools, assessments, knowledge modules and some other helpful tools. The rest of this overview chapter gives you a quick tour of everything that is contained in your new Campus ToolKit system.

Knowledge Modules *(Start here.)*

We've already mentioned our online knowledge modules – and these are a great place to start if there's something you need to know. These aren't dry, boring, textbook-type blocks of information, but real life help with the challenges that college students face.

Things like:

- ~ Comprehensive test-taking help and tips
- ~ Secrets to studying smart and saving time
- ~ Concentration busters and how to avoid them
- ~ Shortcuts to better memorization and information retention
- ~ Solid techniques for avoiding procrastination
- ~ Overcoming Anxiety
- ~ Goal setting for students
- ~ Help with time management
- ~ Money management
(Yes, even for the extremely financially challenged)...

... and a lot more.

Campus ToolKit System Orientation
First up under Knowledge Modules is the system orientation. This takes you on a tour of Campus ToolKit and explains how the whole thing works. Give it a try now if you want to, or, read on.

Assessments
Assessments are the heart of Campus ToolKit. This is how we are able to base our advice on your individual personality type. Even though we have varying shades of personality traits, we all have a base personality type, and natural tendencies. However, it can sometimes be difficult to figure out what type you are!

Here are some examples:

> Brianna loves to stay up talking animatedly until all hours of the night with her friends, but when it comes to a classroom situation, she is usually quiet and reserved. She loves spending time with her family and her existing friends, but doesn't really find it so easy to make new friends.
>
> At home, John is all business. He has studying to do, chores to complete, and doesn't have a lot of time (or the interest) to sit around

> chatting with his family. However, at school he gets to express himself. He loves to talk with friends, frequently dominates classroom discussion, and is considered to be one of the funniest guys around.

Although these are opposite behaviors, both Brianna and John exhibit them at different times. So if you exhibit contrasting behavior patterns or personality styles, which is the *"true"* you? The way to find out for sure is to do our online assessments. When you have completed them, you'll understand a lot more about who you really are.

Our assessments aren't *all* about personality. Here is a quick list of our assessments, and what they do. We have placed them in an order in which they make sense to complete, but feel free to take them in any order. You may find it helpful to complete them before you read chapter three (which is where we'll begin referring to your personal traits) but again, this book is designed so that you can dip in and out of any chapter that may be grabbing your interest at the time.

Locus of Control assessment
This chapter is all about how you see things. You, personally. By taking the short Locus of Control quiz, you'll get an idea of where you place YOU in the whole scheme of your life. Do you make things happen? Or do things seem to happen to you? This is important information to know. How you view your ability to control your own destiny plays a vital role in your success in college. It is also critical in determining your overall level of happiness in life!

Sensory Learning Styles assessment
This is an assessment to complete as soon as you can, because it gives very specific insight to your learning style. Your learning style is how you learn most effectively, and it is key to your success in college. Are you a visual learner? Or do you learn by hearing something? Maybe you're a tactile or kinesthetic learner, who learns best by doing or by immersing yourself in a task.

There is no time to lose academically, so the sooner you understand what your learning style is, the sooner you'll discover your own secrets to better learning skills and more effective studying.

Throughout this book and our online Knowledge Modules you'll see specific tips for your learning style. For example,

> **Concentration for Auditory Learners**
> Auditory learners are very well suited to group discussions and study groups. If you find you are having a hard time concentrating in your usual study environment, try organizing study groups, so that you have more chances to *"hear"* information. You may actually have an easier time studying with others rather than isolating yourself in a quiet environment.
>
> When your mind starts to wander, try speaking important points aloud, recording them, and playing them back.

In order to get the most out of this personalized information, it is probably a good idea to take each assessment before you read the chapter that discusses it.

Study Skills assessment
This assessment gets right to the heart of where you're excelling when it comes to general study skills, and where you could improve. This may seem obvious, but most often we're not even aware of our challenges. This assessment will make you re-think where you study, how you study, and your whole attitude about college.

We've taken the assessment a step further, and added information about how you can work with your own personality type to improve your study skills.

This assessment covers everything from how your brain actually processes information to how to get the right information from your instructors, including what is going to be on their tests!

Communication (DISC) assessment
Now we're talking. This assessment is about your behaviors and communication style. Once you take the short assessment and discover what your own behaviors are, you can learn how to connect better with other people. How can you communicate most effectively with those around you, especially if they're not the same type as you are? This assessment is the first step toward understanding your own personality and behaviors and how to get the best

out of others. You'll *really* be on fire when you combine it with the PLSI, which we'll talk about next!

Personality (PLSI) assessment

This assessment gives you a more in-depth look at your personality. Whereas DISC and communication are about behaviors, personality is about inherent traits that we all have. Once you can identify your own personality type, you can start to spot tendencies in those around you – like your parents, roommates, instructors and friends. This is a very enlightening tool. Many people don't start to get a natural feel for this information until mid-life. It's a major shortcut to understanding how to get along with more people with a lot less strife.

Job Interest Profiler assessment

After answering some questions, this assessment will give you an idea of what your vocational interests are. If you aren't quite sure what you want to do for a career, this is where you can narrow down your ideas and get some direction. Not only does this assessment give you accurate feedback on what you'd be into, it also gives you examples and information on over 900 occupations, and shows those that fit you best.

This means you can explore these careers and choose a major that will work for you in the long run (or learn more about the one you have chosen). You can even save profiles of the careers you're considering.

Work Importance assessment

Working hand-in-hand with the Job Interest Profiler, the Work Importance exploration tool helps you figure out what is important to you in a job. Do you like to get group recognition of your efforts, or would you rather work alone? Would you rather have a steady job that you didn't need to worry about, or unlimited opportunity for advancement? Is it more important that you get to try out your own ideas at work, or would you rather belong to a finely-tuned team?

For every combination of work values, there are jobs to match - and they're all ready and waiting for you to discover in this assessment.

Financial Awareness assessment

This is the stuff we should all know, but admittedly, many of us don't! A lot of financial awareness comes about only when you experience something for the first time, and often the bigger lessons occur only when something goes wrong! And yet, these are issues we all will certainly face in life, including:

~ Cars and car payments, and why an expensive car can be the dumbest investment you'll ever make - *especially* in college!

~ The scoop on hidden charges you might be paying at your bank.

~ How credit cards can cost you *way* more than you thought they would.

~ How to access your money when traveling abroad.

~ The ins and outs of health insurance.

~ How over the next 30 years you can painlessly save 15 million dollars.

~ Why credit companies keep track of your history.

~ The secret of budgeting and *always* having the money for what's. important to **you**.

Start with our pre-quiz, which is a fun way to check your financial savvy. If you find you need a little guidance, it's all here in the book and online. After reading up, try the post quiz and see how much more you know!

The Tools

Once you've finished your assessments, check out our collection of tools. This is where you can really fine-tune your time management, goals, and budgets. We also give you quick ways to communicate with various personality types, including the dynamics of teams and groups. Many of these will mean a lot more to you when you've learned about yourself and others by taking the assessments, and they are online for you to use any time.

Getting in touch

Because this is a book about **you**, the first person we recommend getting in touch with is, well ... *you*. That's why we've designed the set of tools right up at the top of your screen. With a notebook and eFolio, you can use your laptop in class and have assignments always at the ready. We've also given you to-do lists, reminders, and a calendar to help you schedule and organize your whole life. Not only that, but you can get in touch with the inner you using your own journal and goal-setting section.

Knights in Shining Armor: Getting Help

Sometimes you need a little bit more help than journaling will provide. Ever feel like life has run you over, backed up, run over you again and peeled out as a final insult? Next time you feel like that, or even if you are only having a minor problem, head to this chapter. It's at the back, like most troubleshooting manuals. We promise, no *"To start, open book"* here. Only a simple list of what can go wrong, and where to find help.

So, that gives you a pretty thorough run-down on the Campus ToolKit system. We didn't discuss every single feature, but we thought it would be best to let you discover a few things on your own.

Flash Point!

Finally, as you go through this book, you may notice our little Flash Points! These notations serve to highlight information we think is particularly important to you. When you see them, we would suggest asking yourself why we think the point is so important and what it means to you. One way to do this is to make a journal entry online, write in the margins, or make a note in the area we've provided at the back of the book. Copy the Flash Point (this will help you remember it) and then just write a few words about its meaning to you individually.

~ Chapter One ~
Through the Wardrobe: Making the Transition to College

Depending on who you are, where you're from, and what your personal circumstances are, you'll most likely be faced with a multitude of interesting challenges during your transition to college. You might even think of more interesting words than "*interesting*" to describe the challenges once you're faced with them! (Feel free to write some of your own descriptions anywhere in this book - but for now, let's stick with "*interesting.*")

For recent high school grads

If you're transferring directly from high school, you might be surprised to discover just how different college is. Don't worry – most of the changes are good ones! Our mission is to give you the heads-up on what's different, and how you can sidestep the usual difficulties experienced by first-year college students.

For Returning Adult Students

If you are a returning student, your transition into college can be even more complicated.

- **If working full time,** you can expect college to take up the majority of your spare time. However, with careful planning and the right attitude, that time can be one of the most exciting and life-changing experiences you'll ever have.
- **If working part time,** you'll have to deal with arranging class times around work, commuting back and forth to campus, and balancing the energy you have available for work and school. Don't forget to schedule in time for fun!
- Of course, **if this is your first time attending college,** all of the high school transition challenges apply to you, too.
- **If you have a family,** you'll have to keep a close eye on time management - family members and friends might have a hard time understanding that **you have another priority in your life now.**

What's so different?

Let's start by talking about some of the differences between high school and college, and what they mean for **you.**

Freedom – for better or worse

The biggest difference you can expect between high school and college by far is freedom. Gone are the days when someone else was responsible for you, and no longer will roll call precede every class (this doesn't mean your instructor won't notice your absence, though.) You can come and go at will, and most likely, nobody will even follow up on you or check on you.

Keep in mind that in college this freedom means taking responsibility for yourself. It means taking responsibility for your time, your actions, and for your education.

Freedom = Responsibility

Sound great? It really is. Being totally responsible for yourself is liberating, exciting, and downright fun. College is also a great training ground for future employment, and that includes *self-employment*. This is where you'll hone your knack for time management, discover or develop your inner motivation, and begin learning skills that will enable you to earn a living doing something of your choice.

But changes aren't always easy to assimilate, especially so many at once. Many students experience difficulties adjusting to this *"whole new world."*

Academics & Study Skills
Here's what we hear most often from students:

"This was so easy for me in high school."

Academically, college is a lot tougher than high school, especially if you've been one of the lucky ones that didn't *really* need to study. If this is you, then listening in class might have been sufficient to do really well; and when you did have to crack a book, you probably didn't need to read it more than once - and maybe only needed to scan headlines and sub-headings.

That isn't going to work in college.

One of the most common challenges faced by incoming college students is that they never really developed high-level study skills in high school. Students who had to work hard and discover their own methods for studying in high school are going to be at a great advantage. If *that* describes you, congratulations!

However, if you skated through classes in high school and still did well, most likely your days of coasting are over. That's great! Because you're in college to get an education, and will learn a lot more by being challenged. Learning more efficient ways to study will be no problem - we'll give you everything you need to know right here in this book.

Learning all new study skills
Campus ToolKit is packed with features to help you learn new study skills. To begin with, it's important to acknowledge that we're all different, and a study method that works for one person might fail miserably for another. So how to learn what works for you? We've written an entire chapter to help you find the best study methods for you, personally, later in the book. Before that chapter, you'll get the opportunity to participate in several fun, easy self-discovery assessments that will teach you a lot about yourself, and help you construct exactly the type of study plan that will guarantee your success in college.

There are too many differences academically between high school and college to list them all, but here are the biggies that we think you should know about:

Academically, it might not be so easy to stand out in a crowd
Why? Unlike high school, where enrollment and attendance were mandatory, most people are in college by choice. Everybody here wants to learn, and that makes people work harder. This overall attitude evens the score when it comes to academic abilities.

Beyond that, if you attend a competitive school with strict entry requirements, your fellow students will be the best of the best. This tends to level the playing field considerably.

Staying on top of studies requires more work
Assignments are different in college.

For example:

> In high school, class lectures often follow the book. Lectures, reading and assignments are given in bite-sized chunks for you to learn with ease. Each day, you may be required to read a short assignment. That same material is usually discussed in class, effectively giving you two *"lessons"* for all material.
>
> In college, lectures are often only on material that is not covered in your book. You are then assigned lengthy material to read, and it is up to you to correlate the in-class lecture with your book material. Your instructor may not explain how they work together.

This means you'll have to make extra effort to **read assigned material**. If you fall behind, you'll make mountains of work for yourself when it's time to catch up.

Tests are cumulative

In high school, once you were tested on certain material, you usually didn't have to worry about being tested on it again. This means you could cram for your exam, memorizing the material for a few days - or hours - and then you could forget most of it again.

In college, tests can be on any material from a semester. Ideas build on each other, so that you develop a deeper knowledge about a subject. The plan is to make new information meaningful to you, so that it becomes part of your working knowledge.

We've got a whole section online giving you suggestions on how to do this. But for now, just clock it as another main difference.

Staying on top of studies

The main way to avoid any of these difficulties is to stay current with your studying. A good ballpark figure for study time is two to three hours per credit. So, if you're in a three credit class, that's somewhere between six and nine hours a week. If you're taking a full load of fifteen credits, that means you'll have up to forty-five hours a week of studying. You can see how getting behind can quickly make catching up difficult.

Let freedom wait

This is one of the areas where your newfound freedom can backfire. If you've planned on studying all afternoon, but it's sunny and your friends are hanging out or playing ball, ask yourself how many study hours you'll be down by taking the afternoon off. Three? Four? Is it realistic that you'll come back at six and start studying, or will the afternoon lead to an evening of fun and no studying? So then how many hours are you down? Six? Or eight?

Where and when will you get those hours back?

We call this idea *"Stealing from Yourself"* and we talk more about it in Chapter Five: Time Management.

No reminders - read the syllabus.
"Don't forget, test on Thursday. Read chapters 14 & 15 and be sure you know..." Does this type of reminder sound familiar from high school? These friendly reminders will be a distant and quaint memory soon.

Most instructors in college will give you a syllabus the first day of class. A syllabus is an outline of what will be covered in the course, in what order. It tells you clearly what to read before each class session, when assignments are due, and when tests will be given.

Once an instructor passes this out, they know **you** know what's coming. They most likely won't give you any thoughtful reminders of what you should be doing.

Your instructor may not remind you, but we can!
Campus ToolKit is full of online tools that can help you manage your study time and remind yourself of what's coming. Calendars, reminder functions and study time estimators abound. If you think you'd like to get a head start on any of these helpful functions, just refer to the System Orientation online, where you'll see a great list of features and how to use them in the Campus ToolKit system.

Missed a class? Deal with it yourself.
If you miss a class or classes in college - for any reason - it's your responsibility to get the lowdown on what you've missed from your fellow classmates. Most often, your instructor cannot take the time to fill you in, and will not have notes to give you on the lecture you missed. Your classmates will though, so be sure to ask for help. You might even make a new friend in the process!

Class sizes can be a lot larger
Most high schools try to keep class sizes to approximately 30 students. This is so your teacher can give you the one-on-one attention you may require.

In college, you might be in a classroom with over 100 students, and required introductory classes may hold several hundred students at a time.

This can make it difficult to approach your instructor – they can appear less human, and more intimidating, like approaching a public speaker. You also might feel intimidated by asking a question in class. If so, you can either choose not to be intimidated and boldly ask the question, or you can visit your instructor during scheduled office hours.

Getting to know your instructors

Even in large classes, it's a good idea to get to know your instructor a little bit. Whatever concerns or questions you may have, there is a good chance they've encountered them before. They are an invaluable resource for information.

One great way to get to know your instructor is to sit up front, and in the center of the class, so that they can at least be familiar with your appearance and your performance in class.

Another reason to get to know your instructor is that someday you might need a letter of recommendation. Wouldn't it be nice to actually have developed relationships with your instructors, so that they truly know you and are pleased to help?

Finally, getting to know your instructors will help you understand what is important to *them*, and can help you discern what material might be on tests, as well as subjects that will be of particular importance in your career.

Instructors aren't necessarily *"teachers"*

Your high school teacher had one job: to teach you. Your instructor or professor in college may have other equally important duties, like conducting groundbreaking research and running labs – not just lecturing.

Your high school teacher was trained to teach, but your instructor was hired because he or she is an expert in a particular field. If they happen to be a good teacher, that's a bonus. Why not let them know you feel that way and make their day (or week)? However, if you find that your professor's teaching style isn't working for you, you'll have to try harder, find better ways to listen. Your job is to find a way to learn from them - not to be *taught* by them.

Meeting with your instructor

When you need to speak with instructors, check your syllabus. Their office hours will be listed there, and during office hours is when it's acceptable to ask questions, discuss ideas or problems with them.

Flash Point!
Did you know that it is even acceptable to discuss what material may be expected on a test?

To learn more about this, check out *Chapter Six, Excelling in the Classroom*, or visit our online Study Skills Knowledge Module and read Self-Testing and Test Strategies.

Personally speaking

So many people, so little time

There is a good chance your new college has a much larger student body than your high school. This can be both good and bad, depending on your personality:

If you're a really social person, you'll love all the activities college has to offer. However, you might find it difficult to tear yourself away from all the fun to get any serious studying done. Another problem is overbooking your free time. College offers a multitude of extracurricular activities. It can be tempting to get involved in every one that sounds interesting, but be careful that you have enough time to study.

How will you know how much free time you really have? Try using our study time estimator in your online tools. This is a really easy online tool that guides you through all of your activities and shows you in a snap how much extra time you will have available.

At the other end of the spectrum, if you are a bit shy, being around so many people can actually make it harder to meet new friends. In some areas, you may have attended high school with the same friends from junior high or even elementary school. Maybe you haven't needed to make new friends in years! And now, you're faced with a sea of new faces. Everyone is generally rushing around from class to class, or they're buried in a book.

Meeting people and making friends

Breaking through can be easier than you think. We've dedicated two complete chapters of this book to behavior and personality. With the right attitude, we'll have your social calendar full in no time.

One great thing about the switch to college is that, especially with incoming students, it's less cliquish. Many students come from out of town, out of state or from other countries, which shakes things up a little. Most people don't have an existing set of friends, so you're all in the same boat.

The bottom line with meeting new people is: be open, and have a good attitude. A friendly, warm smile can work wonders, for both you and others.

Feeling homesick

It's normal to feel homesick at college. Many times this is your first experience living away from home, which of course can be really hard to deal with. If you've moved away to college, just know that feeling homesick for your friends, family – even missing food and scenery is normal. But, there is usually something good about each new situation - so open up, ask around, meet people and find some nice things about your new town.

What about feeling homesick in your **own** town? It can happen! If you are going to college in your hometown, you might just wish things were as they were, in high school or before you enrolled in college. Your friends might have moved away to attend college, or they may have different priorities now that they've graduated high school. It can feel like your own town is empty. If so, try to focus on this new stage of your life, and what can be good about it. College has a wonderful way of exposing students to interests and experiences they couldn't have imagined possible. We'll discuss how to keep yourself open to these sometimes unnerving, but wonderful, changes later in this book.

Even as a returning student, it would be very normal to feel nostalgic or even regretful about leaving a comfortable job to attend college. You might miss lunches with co-workers, telling jokes on your coffee break, and regular pay. On the up side, choosing to return to college is an important investment in yourself and your future. You chose to enroll for a reason: this might be about a better job or career, more knowledge in your field, or just finishing something you started. Either way, work will *always* be there, but a chance to go to college may not.

Congratulations on making the change and believing in yourself!

Keeping in touch with old friends
Whether your social calendar is so full that it's a burden, or you're staring at the walls every Saturday night, it's important to stay in touch with friends and family. If you're feeling lonely, it reminds you that you have a support network of people who know you and love you. Even if you're loving your new college life, it's good sometimes to talk to people who have known you for a long time. It's a *"keeping it real"* thing.

Don't expect things to continue as they always have though. Most people who have gone through the college experience will tell you that the transition changed things. Relationships with old friends weren't the same, going back home seemed different – both because their focus was somewhere else, but they were also learning to relate to their parents in a new, more adult way. The good news is that these changes aren't bad. Home will always be home and your warm feelings toward the people you went to high school will remain even though you may grow apart.

Just plain responsibility
Getting back to our main difference between high school and college, there are many aspects of college that require you to just plain take responsibility.

High school is a time of following the rules, and - for many - breaking rules when you can. Rules in high school are clear, and rules are not supposed to be broken. When you broke a rule and got caught, you were usually corrected or got some form of punishment. When you broke rules and got away with it, it was probably seen as a positive thing by you.

In college, there are fewer rules, and they are the same common sense rules you'll face in the real world – in your job, and within your community. When you don't live up to these expectations - like showing up for class, or studying - it's only **you** who pays the price. For example, some instructors won't collect homework or check on your progress, but instead they'll assume you're studying and learning the material. If you're having difficulty, they'll presume you'd visit their office. If you're not asking questions, they tend to think you're doing ok.

Another way college is more like the *"real world"* is in performance standards. In high school, doing your best and trying your hardest counted for almost everything. If you were really trying, your teachers would normally find ways to help you, or give you a passing grade.

In college, trying your best is important, but your grades are what count. It works like the real world: you may be a nice person, but if you can't do your job, you won't be kept on the payroll as a friendly smile or a companion for your co-workers.

Flash Point!
Show up for classes and tests
An average class in college may only have two to four tests. Don't miss one! Make up tests may not be available—you'll have to check with your instructor. The bottom line is, unless there is an absolute emergency, you need to be there.

Same goes for class. Being present (mentally as well as physically!) and on time is important. The majority of your instructor's test questions will probably come from lecture material. If they're saying it, it's probably important. Because of that, look at being in class as an opportunity to attend a free study session—one where your instructor tells you the answers to the test.

Knowing what it takes to graduate
What courses do you need to take? How will you assure that you're on a path to graduation? These questions can be answered by consulting your college catalog or by visiting an academic advisor. However, nobody is going to check on you or point out any mistakes in choices when it comes time to enroll and select classes.

Graduation requirements can change, and can be confusing. If you need direction, it's available… but you'll have to ask.

Graduating when you're a part-timer

A quick word of encouragement to those part-time students who might feel a little discouraged that it's going to take up to seven years to graduate. Here's the thing: seven years will go by whether you're in college or not. In seven years, you'll be seven years older, and you'll either be a person who was too short-sighted to stick it out, or you'll be a person smiling and waving your hard-earned college degree. Either way, seven years will go by. So remember that on dark days when you might think of giving up, and keep at it!

Time management and scheduling

Take responsibility for your time, and for your weekly and daily schedule. We can't stress this enough, because allowing enough study time (and actually studying) is critical to your academic success, and results in a lot less stress.

Dealing with money

This may also be the first time you've had to completely manage your own money. We've dedicated a whole chapter of this book to money, and we have even more help online.

If you need help budgeting your money, try our online budget calculator - you'll find it under the Tools menu. This will give you the straight scoop on your finances.

If you need help finding money, visit our Financial Aid Knowledge Module online, in the Money Management section. Or make an appointment with your financial aid office.

Working

Thinking of getting a part time job for some spending money? Think carefully - you've got a big job already! If there is a way to avoid working, you should consider it, so that you can give your studies your full attention. We discuss this topic at length in Chapter Nine: Managing Your Pot of Gold.

Returning and Part-Time Students

As a returning student, time is especially important.

When considering your course load, we highly recommend performing these simple online exercises before making your decision:

- **Time Estimating Exercise** – How much time do you really have in your day? You'll need to know before committing to classes, and knowing starts with this exercise.
- **Study Time Estimator** – Course loads often look a lot lighter than they actually are. You may be able find time to attend two nighttime courses every week, but can you find 18 additional hours for studying? You'll know the answer when you use this tool.
- **Weekly Time Tracker** – How much time do you really have? If you seem to come up short on time every week, try our weekly time tracker to see where the time went.

Also consider taking full advantage of our online calendars, schedules and reminders. Anywhere you have access to the Internet, they'll be ready and waiting for you to view or print.

Money can also be of particular importance to returning students, because many of you have more financial obligations than the average college student. The budgeting calculator will be an invaluable tool as you plan your finances each semester.

As we said at the beginning of the chapter, there are just too many differences between high school and college to explain the impact of every single one. As you follow through this book and our online system, you'll start to discover exactly how these differences will affect you, and how to make your transition to college as easy as it can be.

The Moral of the Story

Enrolling in college means big changes to your lifestyle, whether you're a returning student or have transferred directly from high school. Overall, college offers a lot more freedom than high school would have. But freedom isn't free. It means taking a lot more responsibility for your time, including academically. It means sharpening your time management skills, and managing your money. It's up to you to balance the fun you can have with the tasks that need to be accomplished. If you don't get your work done, who will?

~ Chapter Two ~
Who's Writing Your Fairy Tale?

We talked in the last chapter about the major differences between high school and college, which (if forced to) we would sum up in this one sentence:

YOU are *now* in control.

Do you believe that? Is it true for you?

If you have taken the Locus of Control assessment, you've scored somewhere between a strong internal locus of control, and a strong external locus of control. If you scored with a strong internal focus, you feel relatively in control of the events in your life. If you scored with a strong external locus of control, your result means that you generally feel that circumstances outside of your control shape your life.

How do you feel about your result? Are you surprised, or was it what you expected? If you are surprised, maybe you'll understand more about why you scored the way you did after reading this chapter.

If you haven't had a chance to take the Locus of Control assessment yet, the test measures how much you believe you control your own destiny, including success, setbacks, and failures. This test is important because:

- ~ People who believe they control their own success or failure in college and in life are typically more motivated to work hard.
- ~ People who believe their success or failure depends upon luck, connections, chance, or fate may be less motivated because they are less likely to believe that their own efforts in life will make a difference in the long run.

Put another way, if you believe your success in life is based on your skills, attitude, hard work and an open mind, you're more naturally going to work hard to develop skills, and live your life with a positive attitude and a mind that is wide open to possibilities.

If you believe your success relies on forces outside of your own behavior or attitude, then you don't have as much of a reason to work hard, might not develop as many skills (what's the use, anyway?) and your attitude may become negative. The final result is a closed mind - when you've already decided that there is nothing **you** can do.

Many of us (whether we like it or not) inherited these beliefs from our parents, families and cultures. If you grew up in a family that believes, *"If it weren't for bad luck, we'd have no luck at all,"* then - like it or not - you might have that belief, even if you don't think about it.

Does your family believe that, no matter how hard you try, you may never get a break? Or does you family believe that becoming a success has little or nothing to do with luck – that it's all about hard work and putting yourself out there?

How does the following statement sit with you?

> *"That's just the way things are."*

How does it make you feel? Does it feel familiar, or does it feel wrong? Do you believe that things just are the way they are? What if EVERYONE thought that, about everything - what would happen or not happen?

It wasn't very long ago that America was still in the throes of the civil rights movement. In 1963, a study was undertaken in a segregated school consisting of an entirely African American student population. Students were asked to sign up for activities during their school break on behalf of the civil rights movement. All of these students, being at a segregated school, would have had an interest in the integration issue. The result was that some students were willing to take part in a march on the state capitol or join a freedom rider's group. Others were only willing to attend a rally - and some avoided even filling out the requested form.

Two years later, another study took place comparing the locus of control of African American civil rights activists to African Americans of a similar education and socioeconomic level who did not take part in such issues. As you might imagine, people who were willing to take part back then - eight years into the fight for equality and still three years from victory - were found to be significantly more likely to have an internal locus of control.

Luck

You might be thinking that some people are just lucky to be born with more money, more connections, and more opportunity. It is certainly true that having connections can help you achieve more in life. However, connections are only that - connections. If someone has connections, it is because they made them. Some people have families or friends with connections. Still, someone had to make those contacts and connections - they put themselves out there, met people, and connected. These are people who made their own opportunities. If they could do it, you can too.

Making your own opportunities is the exact opposite of accepting life's leftovers. Which would you prefer? The choice is yours.

Attitude & Behaviors

"If you think you can or you think you can't, you're right."
— Henry Ford

It takes a lot of motivation to achieve success in college, and your attitude and behaviors are what fuel your motivation.

If you received a high score (more externally focused) in the Locus of Control assessment, it might help to really spend some time thinking about the reasons why college is important to *you*. If you're not sure of those reasons, we'll help you develop them. By finding a way to relate college to your future goals, your attitude will naturally get better. It's easier to have a good attitude about something if you know why you're doing it, and what you're going to get out of it!

Attitude is fluid

Your Locus of Control score was based on how you rated statements like:

1. The primary reason for environmental problems is that people don't take enough personal responsibility.
2. Many of the unhappy things in people's lives are partly due to bad luck.
3. A strong individual has the ability to change the course of history.

Depending on when you took the test, you may or may not still feel the same about your answers. Your attitude is fluid, and can change very quickly based on what is happening in your life, your circumstances, and your level of motivation.

Attitude is a choice

In fact, attitude changes all the time, every moment. That is because attitude is a choice, and not a given. At any moment we can decide how we want to view things. Even when something *"bad"* happens, you have a choice in how to view the circumstances.

For example:
Ever notice how two people can be in the very same room at the same event can have a different experience? That is because their attitude dictates how they feel about and perceive what happens there:

> Let's say, for example, that Mary and Shauna both decide to attend a workshop to learn how to draw with charcoals. Neither Mary nor Shauna know anyone there, but Mary decides to say hello to other people and strike up conversation. She spends the afternoon laughing with new friends and interacting with the instructor. She asks questions and learns a lot.
>
> Shauna decided before she got there that the attendees would all be a bunch of amateurs, and not up to her artistic level. Upon arriving, she sees people talking and laughing and assumes everyone knows each other. She sits at a table by herself, and doesn't get the chance to interact with anyone. She learns very little, but she presumes it's because the class was for beginners.

Both Mary and Shauna could have changed their attitudes at any time, but they would have had to make a **choice** to do so.

Life is

10% Circumstances **90% Attitude**

> *"The real voyage of discovery is not in seeing new landscapes but in having new eyes."*
> — Marcel Proust

Look again at the second example statement from the Locus of Control test:

2. *Many of the unhappy things in people's lives are partly due to bad luck.*

It is pretty hard not to agree with this statement. Of course unhappy things in people's lives are partly due to bad luck. But every day in our lives we have a choice about how we view the events surrounding us. Can you think of examples when bad luck turned out to be good luck in disguise? If so, we'd love to hear about it!

Attitude Exercise

Take a moment to write down the answers to these two questions. Feel free to write right here, in the book! Or you can log in to Campus ToolKit and complete this exercise online. It is located under the Tools > Exercises menu.

What academic subjects do you have a good attitude about?
List the things that cause your good attitude about these subjects.

____

____

____

What academic subjects do you have a bad attitude about?
List the things that are causing a bad attitude.

____

____

____

Here are a few things to consider:

1. Do you like the subject?
    a. If you don't like it, how long ago did you make that decision?
2. Is the course too easy or too hard for you?
3. Is the course relevant to your major or career path?

For each of these questions, try to find things that might help you adjust your attitude about them.

For example, if the course is too easy for you:

~ Focus on how an easy "A" will help your grade point average.

~ Think about having more time to spend on your harder courses.

~ If you really want to go crazy, approach your instructor about doing an alternate project or paper that would push your knowledge beyond the basics of the course. That would really impress the instructor, and help you more in the long run.

Keep your answers to these questions, and consider how you could improve your attitude about these subjects as you read on.

> **Flash Point!**
> Attitude is a reflection of your beliefs
> What you believe is true for you.
>
> *"The mirror reflects the answers we seek."*
> — Marie Cleary

Here is where we get to the heart of the Locus of Control issue. Your attitude will fall in line with whatever you believe.

- ~ If you believe you are bad at math, your attitude about math will tend to be bad.

Whatever we believe, we will find evidence of. Therefore, it will become true for you.

- ~ If you believe you are bad at math, your attitude about math will tend to be bad. As your math course gets more difficult, it will reinforce your belief. Instead of feeling challenged by the material, you will find proof that you're bad at math.
- ~ If you believe that you are good at psychology, you'll tend to enjoy your psychology class, even if the material is really challenging. Therefore, you'll do well in psychology.
- ~ If you believe that nobody likes you, you won't be as likely to open up to new people, and you won't give anyone the chance to know you. Therefore, you might see this as proof of your thought that *"nobody likes you."*
- ~ If you believe college is the opportunity of a lifetime, your attitude will be one of excitement, and you'll choose to look for - and take - opportunities. Because of this belief, college will be the opportunity of a lifetime for you.

Your beliefs about something dictate what your attitude will be, so make sure you don't limit yourself by what you believe! Changing your attitude starts with changing your limiting beliefs.

Flash Point!
Changing your beliefs can change your life.

When training baby elephants, handlers use chains to keep them in one place. Try as they might, the little ones can't break free. As they get bigger, handlers only have to use a thin rope, or even a string, because the elephants have learned - and believe - they can't break free.

Sometimes we can be a little bit like elephants! We decide early on what works and what doesn't, and we stick to our beliefs. But it's never too late to change our minds. When our minds are open to change, we can change our beliefs and attitudes.

Changing beliefs starts with believing in yourself!
Believing in yourself starts when you ***believe*** *yourself.*

Believing in yourself means that you trust yourself, and our trust in ourselves grows when we do what we say we're going to do. Doing what you say you're going to do means:

~ When you enroll in a class, you finish it!

~ When you encounter a problem that seems impossible, you find a way around it.

~ When you attend a workshop or lab, you learn from it.

~ When you tell yourself you'll study all day on Friday, you do it!

~ When you face a difficult task, you keep at it, step-by-step, until it's finished.

Every time we do what we say we'll do, our confidence and belief in ourselves goes up. When we break promises to ourselves, we believe ourselves a little bit less next time.

When you believe in yourself, you give yourself permission to do better, learn more, and grow more. That way, when it's time to learn something new, you feel confident! Not because you know how to do something similar, but because you can count on yourself, and you believe in your ability to learn and follow through. If you meet a problem, you know that you can get past it. You have before, and you will again.

When you are achieving things, your overall attitude gets better!

> *"When you only set out to do what you already know how to do, you never develop a true sense of self-confidence."*
> — Barbara De Angelis

I'll have a better attitude later!
It's easy to think things like:

- ~ School is boring. I'll try harder when I graduate and get a good job.
- ~ I'll have a better attitude when I'm in a class I actually like.
- ~ I would enjoy this class if my instructor were a better teacher!

The truth is that attitude, effort, and trying take practice. You can't just turn them on when you think it's time.

> If you really believe school is boring, then you have a matching attitude that says, *"School is boring."*
>
> This attitude will probably create a lack of enthusiasm and effort in your schoolwork. You might not work hard enough to get good grades, and you won't make a great impression on your instructors. Any paper or thesis you write will probably be boring. With that attitude, there is even the chance that you won't graduate.
>
> When you finally apply for a job that you could enjoy, your grades might not be up to par. Your extracurricular activities won't reflect

the enthused type of person many employers want to hire. You'll probably get poor recommendation letters from your *"boring"* instructors. Or, you might not get the degree required to get the job in the first place.

If you believe school is boring, ok. But ask yourself if that's the way you want to spend your time in college. If it isn't, what can you do about the situation? Can you find a way to challenge yourself? If so - if you can find something that interests you and pursue it - then you would naturally start feeling more enthusiasm, and would put more effort into your work. Your instructors will pick up on your excitement, because your papers will be more thoughtful and interesting. When you finally apply for a job, your grades will be on target, and you'll have something to talk about in the interview.

When one of your beliefs isn't serving you, ask yourself what you can do to change it. How can you replace these negative thoughts into positive ones? How can you make the most of your time, for your own sake?

"The journey and the journey's end are inseparable."

Effort and Commitment

"Why is it that we judge others by their behavior, and ourselves by our good intentions?"
— Irish Proverb

Wanting to do well is not enough. Intending to make changes doesn't bring about change. Actually changing your attitude, doing well in college, and graduating all take commitment – and effort.

What level of effort are you making right now?
Are you really reading and thinking about this book? Or are you just skimming? How did you feel when you read the results of your Locus of Control test? Did you feel positive and excited about improving your attitude? Or did you feel skeptical, or even sarcastic? Did you even care at all?

It's easy to make an effort for something you are excited about. That's why finding your own reasons to be in college and believing in your goals makes it easier to be more enthusiastic about your time here, and stimulates effort and commitment.

The more effort you put in to college, the better your results; results like good grades, satisfaction, excitement, enthusiasm, and achievement. In turn, those good results turn into good opportunities, which generate even more enthusiasm. Once you start practicing this process, life gets better and better!

It's this simple:

- ~ If you're putting in a 50% effort, you'll get 50% results.
- ~ If you put in only 10% effort, or no effort at all, you're left with whatever results circumstance provides.
- ~ **But if you give something your best effort, you'll enjoy much better results.**

However, if your Locus of Control results were very external, you may have a hard time believing this. If so, stop right now. Ask yourself, *"Is this belief working for me?"* Then really think about the following questions again:

- ~ Is it possible that the results you are getting right now are based on your effort, or lack of effort?
- ~ Are your results really tied to your circumstances?
- ~ What would happen if you tried harder?

"If we all did the things we are really capable of doing, we would literally astound ourselves."
— Thomas Edison

Positive Thinking

"All I really had was a suitcase and my drums. So I took them up to Seattle and hoped it would work."
— Dave Grohl, (Nirvana, Foo Fighters, Tenacious D)

Why should you think positively?

Imagine you're on a dream skiing holiday and you stumble, break your leg, and then hit your head on a tree. You arrive in the Emergency Room and in walks the doctor. How would you want the doctor to react? Would you want your doctor to say, "*Just relax and stay calm, we'll have to perform surgery, but we'll find a way to fix it.*"?

Or would you want your doctor to put his hands on his head and yell, "*Your leg is broken in two places! You might never walk again! Your head looks bad, real bad! I don't think I can fix this.*"?

Which doctor is likely to treat your injuries more capably?

Now think about your new life in college. You have dreams of graduating, and starting the life of your dreams. Inevitably, you'll face challenges along the way. Which approach is more likely to solve your problems: "*I'll find a way*" or "*I don't think I can*"?

The way you think controls your attitude, actions, and motivation. Thinking positively is no guarantee that things will go well, but it's your best chance.

When you think positively you focus on possibilities and opportunities. When you think negatively, you focus on what can't happen and what's impossible.

Acting as if

> "*Act the part and you will feel the part. Feel the part and you will BE the part!*"
>
> — Foster Hibbard

Along with changing your attitude, it's important to begin to act as if you are the person you would like to be. This is the "*fake it until you make it*" concept and it works because it gets us through that awkward transition phase between being the person we are now and becoming the person we wish to be.

For example:

If you are always late, and you would like to be the type of person who is always on time - or even early - behave the way you think this type of person might. Would they be more aware of time? Would they leave ten minutes earlier, just to be on the safe side? By being aware of what an on-time person would do and acting like them, you'll start to be on time!

If you would like to be the type of person who is enthusiastic and excited about college, act like you think this type of person would act.

> *"We are what we repeatedly do. Excellence, then, is not an act, but a habit."*
> — Aristotle

When all else fails, SMILE!

Smiling causes a positive, life-affirming chemical and physiological response in our bodies. Our brain floods with happy chemicals, we breathe more easily and blood circulates better! When we are smiling, it's very hard to feel negative. The next time you have a bad attitude or a lack of enthusiasm, just smile in spite of it. You might feel a little goofy at first, but you'll also feel better almost immediately!

Your attitude makes a difference to other people

Imagine it's the first thing in the morning. You start the day by hitting the snooze button too many times, and have to miss your shower and your breakfast.

You're tired of getting up every morning for school, and stressed about being late, so you snap at your roommate and run out the door.

Your roommate is highly annoyed by your snappy comment and is short with his girlfriend on the phone as she is headed to work.

She is so upset and confused by your roommate's behavior that she runs a stop sign and cuts someone off.

That person honks loudly and gets angry. When they get to work they only grumble as the receptionist says hello.

The receptionist then decides that she is sick of being cheerful to rude people and treats everybody who calls that day poorly.

Now let's start the day another way
You set your alarm so that you can get up ten minutes early and enjoy a nice breakfast.

Over breakfast, your roommate gets to run an idea he is excited about past you, and you're able to encourage him and offer positive advice.

He calls his girlfriend on her way to work and arranges to meet her over dinner that night to celebrate his idea.

On her way to work, she is in such a good mood thinking about dinner that she lets someone into traffic.

That person feels happy, because there was a long line of cars. When they get to work, they smile and say, *"Good morning!"* to the receptionist.

The receptionist feels appreciated, and good about her job, and treats everyone who calls that day cheerfully.

Can you imagine how far your good attitude can travel? Each person who was affected then affects many more people. You actually affect thousands, if not hundreds of thousands of people every day by your attitude.

> *"When we try to pick out anything by itself, we find it hitched to everything else in the Universe."*
> — John Muir

The Moral of the Story
In life, attitude counts more than circumstances. Ever wonder why two people in the exact same circumstances can have such different experiences? It's because of their attitudes! If your attitude about something is good, it will be good for you. If your attitude is bad, it will be bad for you. Your attitude is closely related to what you believe… and what you believe will be true for you, because it will affect the amount of effort you put into something. Whatever effort you put in to college is equal to the result you'll get.

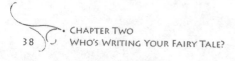

~ Chapter Three ~
Know What You Want Before You Get Your Three Wishes

Why are you here?

Really! Why are you here? We don't mean in the whole scheme of the universe, or because your parents fell in love, we mean, why are you in college? Because, unless you have a clear idea of why you're here, you are going to find it hard to be motivated.

Motivation and attitude start with taking responsibility. In college, you are the only person responsible for your actions. YOU decide whether you go to class or spend the afternoon shopping. YOU decide whether to study or have fun with your friends. YOU decide how you tackle a difficult subject, or whether you let your personal life get in the way of school, or how you deal with a professor.

How much responsibility do you take for your success in school? Do you feel ready to buckle-down and do the hard work needed to graduate? That might be hard to do if you don't have your own personal reasons for being in college. You might be in college just because you're expected to be, or because all of your friends and family went to college. Due to the amount of work it takes to successfully get through college, it's vital to develop your own goals and reasons for getting your degree.

Even if you already **know** that you're in college because of your own reasons - because you really want to be - it's important to be familiar with what motivates you.

Having your own motivations for being in college, and creating personal goals also make your time in college more fulfilling and enjoyable. Instead of taking away from the fun, it allows you to be more enthusiastic, and gives a deeper meaning to your time here.

An old saying applies:

When you care about what you do, enthusiasm carries you through.

Finding your priorities and values

Becoming motivated begins when you discover your priorities and values. Here's an exercise that is useful to help you find and remember what motivates you:

Think about the following questions, and once you have a clear answer in your mind, write the details in the space provided. *There's also a place to do this online if you want. Look for the Priorities & Values Journal under the Tools > Exercises menu.*

If you are only in your first week or so of college, think back to high school courses or general subjects in life. Don't answer the way you *think you should*, answer the way you *really feel.*

1. **What classes do you enjoy?**

   ____

   ____

2. **Why are they enjoyable to you?**
   Is it because you are interested in the subjects, or because you like your instructors in these classes?

   ____

   ____

3. **What originally made you choose to enroll in the subjects you enjoy?**

   ____

   ____

4. **What classes don't you enjoy?**

   ____

   ____

5. **Why aren't they enjoyable to you?**

   ____

   ____

6. **Why did you originally enroll in these subjects?**

   ____

   ____

7. **What are your reasons for staying in the un-enjoyable classes and learning the material?**

   ____

   ____

8. **What are the standards you set for yourself in school?**
   Are these your standards, or someone else's, such as your parent or a coach?

   ____

   ____

9. What drives you to achieve these standards?

10. Do you think these are realistic standards?

11. What are your plans after college?

12. Is a college degree necessary for these plans?

13. If not, is there still value in getting a degree? Remember that most people will have up to five career changes in their life.

14. When work is difficult, what motivates you to continue studying?

15. Why is getting an education important to you?

16. How do you plan to use your education? Is it to get a good job, or to do something you love?

17. What makes getting a degree important to you?

18. How important to you is getting a degree?
Very, somewhat, or not very?

____

____

19. Are these your reasons, or are they someone else's, like a parent or coach?

____

____

20. What do you want to learn in college?

____

____

21. Do you believe you will graduate?

____

____

Your answers to these questions should be enlightening. Can you begin to identify what motivates you to be in school?

> *"Knowledge is power. Information is the source of knowledge."*
> — Anonymous

Intrinsic and Extrinsic Motivators
Whether you are motivated intrinsically or extrinsically is important to identify.

Intrinsic Motivators are internal motivations. For example:

~ Joining the swim team because you'd like to feel more fit.

~ Learning Spanish because you want to backpack through South America this summer.

~ Learning about Eastern Europe because you want to understand your family history.

Extrinsic Motivators come from outside of you. For example:

~ Joining the swim team because everyone expects you to.

~ Learning Spanish because it's required that you learn a foreign language.

~ Learning about Eastern Europe only long enough to get through Friday's test. Who cares about Eastern Europe, anyway?

When you look back over your answers to the questions above, do you feel that you are motivated intrinsically or extrinsically?

For example:
If you've decided that you want to get a 4.0 G.P.A. in college:

An intrinsic reason is because you want to know that you completely understand all the material you are learning and master each subject. Or maybe you are planning to attend a very competitive graduate school, and your heart is set on getting into this school.

An extrinsic reason would be that your Dad gets disappointed when you don't get straight A's, or your family will be disappointed if you don't get in to the graduate school of your choice.

Why identify intrinsic and extrinsic motivators?

> *"The best guarantee of a man's success in his profession is that he thinks it is the finest in the world."*
> — Anonymous

In general, if you have intrinsic motivations, you'll have more of a drive to meet your goals. Students who are intrinsically motivated to enroll and complete college usually:

~ Work harder to achieve their academic dreams

~ Put more effort into their schoolwork

~ Find ways around problems and challenges

~ Exercise the self-discipline necessary to do well in school

Extrinsic goals *work*, but intrinsic goals ***work better***.

If you return to your answers to the questions in the priorities and values journal, try to identify intrinsically and extrinsically motivated answers.

Which types of motivation do you see more of? Is there any way to turn extrinsic motivators into intrinsic ones? Can you find an intrinsic benefit to your courses and activities that you haven't thought of before?

Discovering Priorities and Values

When you can identify your extrinsic and intrinsic motivators, you're close to discovering your priorities and values. Values are your core beliefs - what matters most to you. Priorities are the parts of your life that you decide come first, based on your values.

To identify your values and priorities in college, try asking yourself the following questions, and write your answers down.

1. **What do I want to *do* in college?**
   Think about what you'd like to do while you're here? Run for class president? Learn to speak Japanese? Get good grades?

   ____

   ____

2. **What do I want to *have* in college?**
   Think about things you want? A nice car? A girlfriend or boyfriend? A dog? A part-time job?

   ____

   ____

3. **Who do I want to *be* in college?**
   Think about how you would want people to describe you to answer this question. Honest? Compassionate? Fun?

   ____

   ____

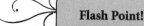

Flash Point!
If the answers aren't coming to these questions easily, it's worthwhile to appreciate that this is *big stuff*. Many people don't think about their motivations in life until they feel things have gone wrong, and some people will *never* put this much thought into their lives. The fact that you do puts you years ahead of most people, and it will pay off big time.

Conflicts

When you have your answers, take a look to see if there are conflicting desires. Conflicts are things that will create a problem for you, or will get in the way of something else you want to do, have, or be.

For example, if you want a nice car, and you want to get good grades, make sure you don't have a conflict. Will you have to work so much more to pay for a nice car that it will hurt your grades?

If you find a conflict, determine your priority
If you get good grades, you'll get your degree and a good job that will pay for a nice car… and you'll have more time for fun in college without a big car payment!

Becoming motivated begins when you begin to align yourself with your priorities and values. Yes, you can skip right to the goal setting if you want to; but your goals will be a lot more fulfilling and purposeful - and you'll be a lot more likely to achieve them - when they are unified with your values and priorities in life.

Write your mission statement
Now that you are starting to get an idea of what your values and priorities are, the next step is to write a mission statement. A mission statement is a short written expression of your purposes and values – kind of like your own personal philosophy on how you want to live.

So why not give it a try? We've got a special tool online to guide you step-by-step through making a mission statement. Once written, it will always be visible when you are logged into Campus ToolKit!

If you're not sure you're ready to commit to a mission statement, just try one for now - you can always go back and change it later if you want.

> *"If you don't set your goals based upon your Mission Statement, you may be climbing the ladder of success only to realize, when you get to the top, you're on the WRONG BUILDING."*
> — Steven Covey, 7 Habits of Highly Effective People

Goal Setting and the Three Golden Rules

> *"I always knew I wanted to be someone. I realize now I should have been more specific."*
> — Lily Tomlin's Bag Lady

Now that you have identified your priorities and values, you can get to work on making some real goals. Goals, even small ones, are the backbone of college success. You might have a long-term goal of earning $600,000 per year, and a short-term goal of concentrating and studying next week's material.

Flash Point!
You can create any goals you want – but to make them work they need to follow the Three Golden Rules: they must be *specific*, *measurable*, and they need to have *deadlines*.

1. Give yourself deadlines

Deadlines are critical to goals. They enable you to create an action plan, and sub-goals.

Not so effective:	I'm going to try sushi.
More effective:	I'm going to eat sushi tonight for dinner!
No so effective:	I'm going to learn to play the piano.

More effective: I'm going to learn to play the piano by June 15th by practicing three times a week and hiring a tutor.

2. Get specific!

"Figure out what you want. I don't mean generally... specifically. Super specifically. And then go do it. That's my motto."
— Jack Black

Try this multiple-choice question:

Getting specific allows you to:

- ○ A. Envision more clearly what you want.
- ○ B. Determine when you're getting closer to what you want.
- ○ C. Easily identify opportunities when they come your way.
- ○ D. All of the above.

The answer should be pretty obvious: it's *d. All of the above.*

Here's how it works:
Let's say you currently have the following goal:

~ **Get a degree and get a good job.**

It's hard to find something to focus on, or look for opportunities with a goal that vague. By spending some time thinking about what you really want, you can come up with a more specific goal, like this one:

Get my degree in Marine Biology by (date) and start a career working with marine mammals.

Now you have something to grab a hold of!

With a goal this specific, you can do many things in college to bring yourself closer to success:

- ~ Use every paper you write, every report, oral presentation, and dissertation as an excuse to learn more about this field.
- ~ Use your research as a great excuse to make connections with those working in the field. These are the people who may eventually hire you! Aim high!
- ~ Having a specific goal allows you to verbalize and share your goal. If your friends, family and instructors know what you want, they can help you.
- ~ Any opportunity in this field that is offered to students at your college will be immediately reported to you, or will stand out when you see it.
- ~ You'll be the best candidate because you've focused so specifically on this subject.
- ~ When it's time to apply for a job, you'll be able to reference all your research, and demonstrate a commitment that will put you ahead of other applicants.

"People with goals succeed because they know where they are going. It's as simple as that."
— Zig Ziglar

3. Make your goals measurable
Having measurable goals means that you know when you're finished.

For example:
If you had a goal to *"Get better grades,"* when would you know you had achieved your goal?

Bringing an *F* to a *D* is better, but is it what you had in mind?

You could make your goal measurable (and more specific) by saying you'll raise your G.P.A. to at least a 3.5 overall. Now you know when to celebrate! Oh, and make a new goal, of course.

Goal Setting Tool
Based on your values and priorities, it's time to create some goals.

Most of us want the same things in life, believe it or not:

- An exciting career
- More money
- Good health for ourselves, and everyone we care about
- To be attractive
- To have meaningful relationships with people
- To own nice things
- Nice vacations
- To feel happy
- To know that we contribute and that we're important
- More time to enjoy the good things in life

From these basic needs we each have our own personal spin. Your unique goals are based on your values, priorities, and your mission statement.

The 5 areas of goal setting

Goals can generally be categorized into five areas of life:

- Money
- Career (this includes college)
- Health
- Relationships
- Spirituality

In each area, decide on your goals. We recommend starting with **just one** major goal in *one area.*

If you really want to do more than that, try to keep it to no more than three at one time. Try: One short-term goal (within the next 3 months), One medium-term goal (within the next year) and one long-term goal (career, lifetime, etc.)

If you have too many goals, you won't be able to focus on them all. You should be able to easily memorize your goals so that you can keep them in mind at all times. In fact, you might want to write them on a sticky note and post them somewhere until you have them memorized.

By the way, don't rip yourself off with small, safe goals. Think big! Just make sure your goal is realistic.

> *"A ship in harbor is safe - but that's not what ships are for."*
> — John A. Shedd

Being realistic

Separating the dreams from the goals.

> *"The foolish person seeks happiness in the distance; the wise person grows it under his feet."*
> — James Oppenheim

When you set your goals, make sure they are realistic. For example, currently there is no *"King of The World"* position available – that's a dream. Creating sub-goals and evaluating the steps you'd need to take will help you determine if your goals are realistic.

Being Specific

Know what you want and you'll get what you want!

> *"The world stands aside and lets pass the man who knows whither he is going."*
> — Ordway Tead

Flash Point!
It's impossible to get what you want if you don't know what you want. Let's repeat that point, because it's important: **It's impossible to get what you want if you don't know what you want.**

The more specific you are – the more details you can imagine, the easier it will be for you to succeed.

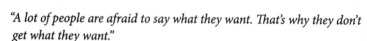

"A lot of people are afraid to say what they want. That's why they don't get what they want."
— Madonna

Taking Action

Effort and Action

"An ounce of action is worth a pound of theory."

Question: Five frogs are sitting on a log.
Four decide to jump off. How many are left?

Answer: Five.
Why? Because deciding and doing are not the same thing.

— Children's Riddle

The next step after deciding what you want and creating a specific goal, is *ACTION*. Without action, nothing happens! All the great ideas in the world can't beat one average idea that is acted upon.

"The most important key to achieving great success is to decide upon your goal, and launch, get started, take action, move."
— Brian Tracey

Cycles of achievement

Attitude, achievement, motivation, and effort are all interconnected. As any one part increases, so do all the rest. This can work positively, like this:

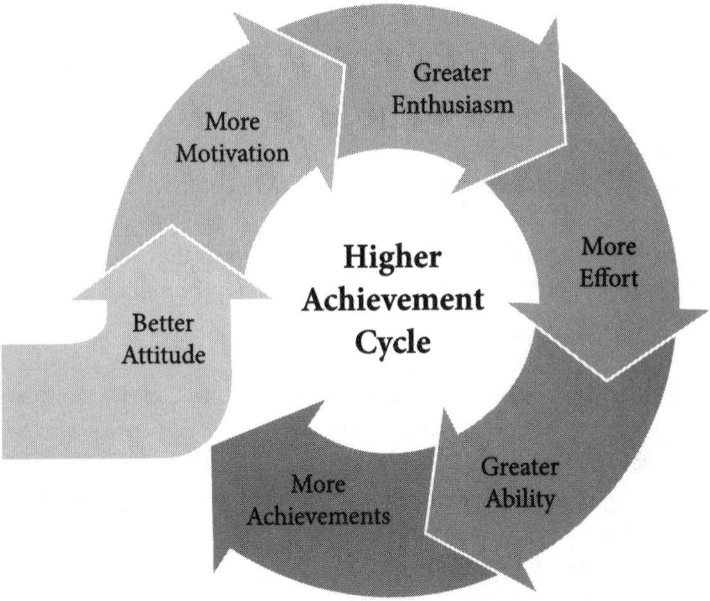

Or negatively like this

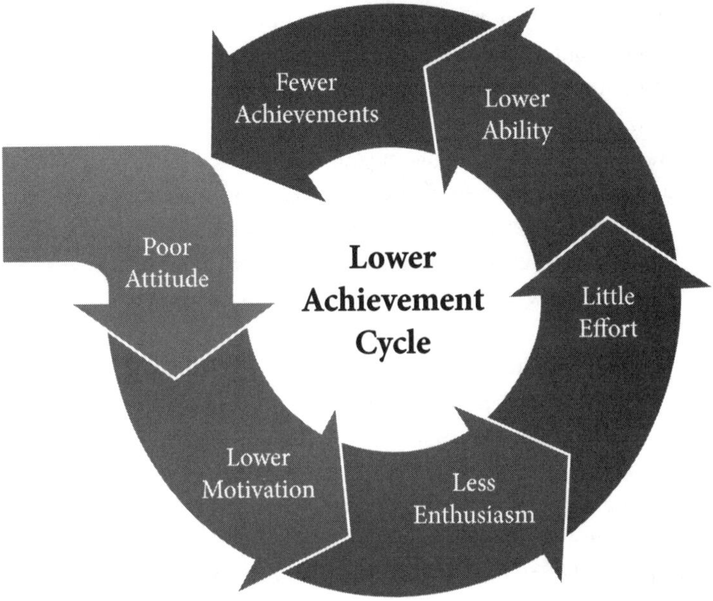

The effort you put into something is the result of your attitude. A good attitude increases your motivation and gives you enthusiasm, which in turn fuels your efforts.

Action and Confidence

Action also brings about confidence. *True confidence.*

Before we begin to talk about how confidence affects the cycles of achievement, let's define confidence. We often confuse ego with confidence, and they are polar opposites.

> **Egotistical behavior:** Bragging, talking up your abilities to other people, and having a superior attitude toward others. People with egos believe in their ability to do certain things well (athletics, driving a nice car, having a good job, dating attractive people). Because of this, they constantly try to prove themselves and compare themselves to others. When you're around a person with an ego, you often start to feel worse about yourself.
>
> **Confident behavior:** Confident behavior is rooted in having a positive attitude about yourself; believing in yourself and others. Confidence is not about knowing something or doing something well. It's not about something you have achieved in the past.
>
> It's about always believing in your ability to learn. It's being able to depend upon yourself. Confidence is having trust that you'll do whatever it takes to achieve something, one step at a time, mistake after mistake, until you get better. When you're around a person with true confidence, you often feel better about yourself.
>
> *"The thing always happens that you believe in. And it's your belief in the thing that makes it happen."*
> — Frank Lloyd Wright

Most of the time, the reason we don't try new things or turn a dream into a goal is because we don't believe in ourselves. We say things like *"Oh, I don't know if I could do that..."* or *"I don't think I can do that."*

Every time you take a step forward, and take action, your confidence and belief in yourself will improve. And confidence is what enables you to try new things, believe in yourself, and live life closer to your dreams.

So start with anything – even a baby step. Be patient with yourself while you get better and better at something and your ability improves.

Nothing ignites your attitude like achievement; especially achievement that follows on the heels of repeated failed attempts!

Ok, time for action!

Now you're ready to use our powerful goal-setting tool; you'll find it in your Tools online. It's easy and we guide you step-by-step through the process. We give you a place to include all the steps you'll need to achieve that goal. When you're finished, you can print your goal or save it online for updating.

"But I can't decide!"

> *"Indecision and delays are the parents of failure."*
> — George Canning

Struggling with indecision can be very frustrating. Worse than frustrating, it can be debilitating. The fear of making the *"wrong decision"* can keep us from making a move for years, or even a lifetime!

Sometimes the reason we can't decide is because we forgot about our dreams, or our dreams were put aside for us, a long time ago. Our dreams are a reflection of who we are. Dreams are maps to finding what we want, and what we feel passionate about.

It's important to listen to your dreams to find something you want to do – something you can feel enthused about. When you're doing what comes naturally – doing what you love - it's easier to be happy.

Doing what you love starts with believing it's possible. If you think it would be fun to work with animals, but you're studying accounting because it's practical, it's worth finding a way to work with animals – even if it's just in your spare time. If you really love it, you can make a change!

This is where your attitude and beliefs reflected in the Locus of Control assessment from Chapter One can be very important. If you don't believe you are in control of your destiny, you won't have an easy time living a fulfilling life.

> *"I dream for a living."*
> — Steven Spielberg

The **key** is to listen to yourself and get in touch with what you naturally love. **Turning the key** is when you decide to actually try something… anything!

> *"Indecision is fatal. It is better to make a wrong decision than build up a habit of indecision. If you're wallowing in indecision, you certainty can't act - and action is the basis of success."*
> — Marie Beynon Ray

About indecision…
Although you may think you are just *"not choosing,"* the fact is that when you allow yourself to be stalled by indecision, ***you are choosing*** - to deny yourself the excitement of success.

The fastest way to knowing what you really want is to make a choice, and try something.

"Get busy living, or get busy dying," says Stephen King (who gets busy writing every day of the year except Christmas, 4th of July, and his birthday).

So pick an option and get going!
This may sound like superficial advice, but the fact is, there is no shortcut or magic solution to deciding. If you suffer from having too many ideas, or being excited about too many things to decide on just one, review the facts and pay attention to your intuition – your gut instinct. Pick one option, and get moving! If a nagging voice keeps reminding you that *"anything could happen,"* or *"No matter how hard you try, sometimes things just don't work out,"* thank that voice for sharing, and keep working toward your dream or goal. YOU are the key to your success.

Using intuition to help you decide

Intuition, or your gut instinct, can play a big part in the decision-making process. It's your gut that often tells you when you're making a decision based on the wrong reasons; fear, addiction, greed, insecurity, true danger to yourself, or the undue influence of others.

Making a decision

1. Look at the facts that are available to you.
2. Get more facts if you feel you need them. Put a deadline on the amount of time you will spend fact-finding.
3. Pay attention to your gut instinct. It can often guide you to the best option.
4. Choose one and get moving!

"The risk of a wrong decision is preferable to the terror of indecision."
— Maimonides

Thinking Positively

Once you determine that your goals are realistic, it's important to think positively and believe that you can achieve them! Nothing undermines a goal more quickly than your lack of belief in it.

Someday Isle

"It's easy to sit there and say you'd like to have more money. And I guess that's what I like about it. It's easy. Just sitting there, rocking back and forth, wanting that money."
— Jack Handey, Deep Thoughts

This humorous excerpt by Jack Handey unfortunately illustrates a mindset many people have – especially those living on *"Someday Isle."*

You'll hear a lot of motivational speakers talk about this phenomenon. Many people live their whole lives on Someday Isle, and it sounds like this:

Someday I'll … Get a degree.
Someday I'll … Go back to school.
Someday I'll … Make more money.

Someday I'll ... Find a perfect career.
Someday I'll ... Volunteer my time at a local organization.

The trouble is, when you're on Someday Isle, you are surrounded by other people on Someday Isle. It starts to seem normal, and acceptable to live your life this way.

It's not
Wave goodbye to all the other people living this way and get off the island right now, by taking action.

Why you should start working on your goals today
Before he died, Michael Landon reminded us, "*Whatever you want to do, do it now – there are only so many tomorrows.*"

Good ideas are a dime a dozen. And anyone can create a goal and say what they're going to do. The difference between dreamers and people who achieve is that they *take action*. We all have the ability - but only a few of us will actually take the steps. Will you be one of them?

Action ideas

Getting a success buddy
One of the best ways to avoid procrastination and take action on your new goals is finding someone to team up with. Exchange goal sheets, including micro-goals and tasks, and check up on each other! When you know someone is going to ask you if you did your task, it makes it a lot harder to put it off – especially when you know they're doing theirs so that they can report back to you!

Finding a reference model or creating one
To help you achieve your goal, think about attitudes and resources that will help you.

Would it help to be:

~ Confident

~ Open-Minded

~ Patient

~ Determined

~ Calm

~ Enthusiastic

~ Relaxed

~ Assertive?

Now, find somewhere that you have that resource:

> Start with yourself. This method is called transference: Was there a time in the past that you had the attitude? If so, think about how you were feeling, why your attitude was good, and how those same feelings can apply to your current situation. Then, transfer those feelings and abilities onto your new goal.
>
> What about another person? Is there someone you know, or know of, who has achieved your goal already? What about someone who has the attitude and resources it would take? If so, use that person as a reference model. If possible, find a way to discuss your goal with them.
>
> If you don't have either of these, create your own reference model and *act the part*. Consider what it would be like to have the right attitude or resources. How would it feel? How would you act? How would you view things?

A backwards plan
You can use reverse thinking to develop a plan for your goal. Just start with where you want to be, and work backwards. What would it take to get there? Keep asking that question until you end up where you are right now.

Mind mapping
This is a great exercise for times when you might have difficulty getting a plan together or knowing where to start. Mind mapping begins by using the biggest piece of paper you can find and bright colored markers or crayons. First, place your main idea in the centre of the page. From here, let your mind

go free placing any ideas that come to mind somewhere on the page with supporting thoughts.

There are several resources for help with mind mapping online, so take a look if you need some guidance. We've got our own guide under the Tools > Exercises menu.

Self-Discipline and Hard Work

Next comes the hard work. As a general rule, nothing worth having comes easily. So, set and follow clear steps to achievement.

> *"Plans are only good intentions unless they degenerate into hard work."*
> — Peter Drucker

Sacrifice is almost always required in one way or another. Your goal to get a 3.0 in Biology will require a sacrifice of time, because you'll need to spend more time studying. That could mean that you'll be sacrificing fun with friends, depending upon how you arrange your schedule.

Encountering Problems, Overcoming Obstacles

Thomas Edison, whose failures far outweighed his achievements, had this to say: *"Remember, nothing that's good works by itself, just to please you; you've got to make the damn thing work."*

Everyone encounters obstacles when they go after their goals. Problems are part of the process of having goals and achieving anything. The higher your goals and expectations of yourself, the more you can expect to encounter problems and failure. More often than not, they're where your best lessons and ideas come from.

> *"New ideas stir from every corner. They show up disguised innocently as interruptions, contradictions and embarrassing dilemmas. Beware of total strangers and friends alike who shower you with comfortable sameness, and remain open to those who make you uneasy, for they are the true messengers of the future."*
> — Rob Lebow

Obstacles can be:

- Problems
- Scenarios you never saw coming
- Friends or family who don't believe in you or support your dreams
- Situations that seem totally impossible

The bottom line with obstacles is: YOU CAN HANDLE THEM!

When you know and believe you can handle obstacles, you will. People are capable of achieving amazing things when they believe they can.

When problems come up, remember your confidence. Remember your belief in yourself, and decide YOU CAN HANDLE THEM.

> *"The diamond cannot be polished without friction, nor the person perfected without trials."*
> — Anonymous

The rubber band theory
Imagine yourself as a rubber band, hooked to one point (where you are now) and stretching to another point (where you want to be).

Getting started toward your goal is easy. You aren't stretching, you're just traveling.

As you get past the halfway point, things may get a little uncomfortable. You're having to stretch, and change.

As you approach your goal, things get very uncomfortable - almost unbearable. You really have to push hard, and there's a lot more tension than when you started.

This is the point where a lot of goals die. This is where obstacles are at their worst. The easiest thing for you to do here is *stop trying*. Give up.

The *bigger* your dream, the *more* uncomfortable the stretch will be.

The reward for seeing it through, overcoming these obstacles and continuing to stretch is that you reach your goal. The pressure is off, and the hard work is done.

Of course, now it's time to set a new goal, and start again! This time, when things get tough, you'll know it's a natural part of the process, and keep stretching.

Flash Point!

"Many of life's failures are experienced by people who did not realize how close they were to success when they gave up."

— Thomas Edison

Patience, and Delayed Gratification

Yuck! Nobody wants to hear these words. But they are an important part of progress. Delayed gratification is a natural law. You plant, and then you harvest.

Planting seeds

Every bit of effort and action you take is like a seed being planted. Every positive thought is a seed being planted. Your attitude, enthusiasm, and effort are like water for your crop.

And just like planting seeds, what grows is so much more than what you planted! Your rewards for determination usually far exceed anything you could have dreamed possible.

But, it takes patience! You don't plant seeds today and get big, fruit-laden trees tomorrow! You get fruit … later. Plant now, harvest later!

"The harder you work, the luckier you get."

— Gary Player

Determination when things don't work out

"I have not failed. I've just found 10,000 ways that won't work."

— Thomas Edison

When you know or read about successful people, what thoughts do you have about their success? It's common to think that their success was easy, or that they were lucky. Maybe you think they were just in the right place at the right time. What we don't usually hear about is all the challenges they faced, and how many times they failed before they succeeded. We don't hear about the mistakes they made, the moments they used poor judgment, and the many times they had to start all over again. Nobody reports the times they came across obstacles that they didn't know how to overcome.

Most successful people have experienced a lot more failure than they have success. What's different about successful people is that they keep going, and they have confidence in their ability to keep trying, one step at a time, through mistakes, setbacks and failure. They view failure and obstacles as valuable lessons. To a successful person, failure is part of the growth process.

During his career, Babe Ruth made a record-breaking 714 home runs. Nobody remembers the 1,330 strikeouts. The reason he struck out so many times was because, every time, he aimed for a home run.

> *"If I'd tried for them dinky singles I could've batted around .600."*
> — Babe Ruth

When things get tough, think about this Gallup Pole statistic:

~ Two out three Americans do not want to go to work in the morning.

Hard work, patience and determination are the secret to being that third person who DOES want to go to work (or school!). So don't give up on your goals when the going gets tough. If you experience failure, see it as an opportunity to learn and try again.

> *"Talent is cheaper than table salt. What separates the talented individual from the successful one is a lot of hard work."*
> — Stephen King

Don't forget this important lesson from Chapter Two:

What you believe is true for you
Your ability to achieve will fall in line with whatever you believe.

- If you believe you can't get the grades you need to get into graduate school, the belief that you can't severely limits your ability to try.

Whatever we believe, we will find evidence of. Therefore, it will become true for you.

- If you believe college is the opportunity of a lifetime, you'll choose to look for - and take - opportunities. Because of this belief, college will be the opportunity of a lifetime for you.
- If you believe college is a waste of time, you won't be looking for any benefits or opportunities, because you won't believe they exist. Instead, you'll find proof that college is a waste of time, and in fact, you'll waste your time in college.

Still can't get started?
If you've got a list of great reasons why you can't start on your goal, you are probably procrastinating. We've got a whole section on procrastination online under the Knowledge menu, and we'll talk a lot about it in Chapter Five, the time management chapter.

If you *already know* you're a procrastinator, maybe you should get on over to Chapter Five now! Or, check out our online procrastination module. Take your first step away from procrastination and do it now.

The carrot and the kick in the pants
It's natural to think about what the payoff is going to be when you achieve your goal. It's like a carrot dangling in front of you on a string. But sometimes it's important to think about what will happen if you *don't* achieve your goal. How will it feel? Is that ok with you? Is it acceptable? **Are your reasons for giving up good enough?**

Those reasons are what we call the *"kick in the pants."*

The carrot is what **you want.** The kick in the pants is **why you can't stay where you are.**

Overcoming Doubt and Fear

> It was a high counsel that I once heard given to a young person, *"Always do what you are afraid to do."*
>
> — Ralph Waldo Emerson

Fear almost always accompanies growth. So if you're feeling a bit afraid of your goal, it's natural!

Although fear can feel and appear to be very real, the *reality* is that fear is generated in our minds, based on how we choose to view our situations. Because of this, you can train your mind to overcome doubts and fear.

Here are two popular ways of breaking down the word *'fear'* that exposes its lack of reality:

F.E.A.R. = False Evidence Appearing Real

F.E.A.R. = Fantasized Experience Appearing Real

In other words, Fear is ***nothing*** *trying* to act like ***something***!

Fear is very much like darkness

Darkness does not exist. In our solar system, there is light, and only light. When we cut off light, there is an absence – or removal of light. But we don't say things like, *"Gosh, there sure is an absence of light in this location."* We say, *"It's dark out here!"*

When we name it, darkness becomes something. We created the word darkness, but darkness doesn't actually exist.

As creations of our mind, fear, worry and anxiety can be compared to darkness. Darkness is the absence of light; anxiety is the absence of confidence. Fortunately, in the same way that turning on the light in a child's dark bedroom banishes the monsters under the bed, we can learn to banish the monsters inhabiting our fearful minds.

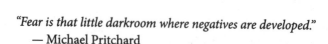

"Fear is that little darkroom where negatives are developed."
— Michael Pritchard

Perfectionism
The best way to learn is by doing. If you wait until you think you'll be perfect to start your goal, you'll probably never start.

Here's a great way that many highly successful people deal with perfectionism:

Ready, Fire ... Aim!

Step 1. Get ready
Step 2. Fire! Get out there and start working, give it a try.
Step 3. Aim. See how you did. Where did you land? How should you change? How can you improve? How far off were you, and how should you adjust your aim?

Put simply: You get ready; shoot the ball; notice where it landed and shoot again.

Don't wait until you feel *"ready."* You'll probably never feel ready until you just ***do it***.

Self-Talk – Controlling what you say to yourself
"We are trampled most often by forces we ourselves create."
— William Shakespeare

All of us have a little voice inside that is constantly telling us something. Many times, it speaks very negatively, using phrases like:

~ I can't handle this

~ If only

~ This is terrible

~ I'll never

~ It's impossible

~ This is too hard

Sometimes the voice can be very aggressive and belittling, saying things like:

- *See, I told you - you wouldn't be able to do it.*
- *How could you think you would be able to do that?!*

The trick to overcoming negative self-talk is to be aware of it, and correct it with positive self-talk. Focus on your capabilities instead of your deficiencies. Looking at some of the items on the list again, let's see what you could say instead:

I can't handle this.	I can learn to handle this.
If only.	Next time.
This is terrible.	This is something I will learn from. Or, what can I learn from this?
It's impossible.	If I really wanted to, I could.
This is too hard.	I can do this if I stick to it.

Remember, the key to overcoming negative self-talk is to begin to recognize when you do it. Chances are, it's a habit and you may not notice all the time. But when you DO notice it, begin to find another way to look at things, a positive way. It'll seem awkward at first, but the more you do it the more this positivity will become a new habit.

Another way to view fear

> *"Freedom doesn't mean having no fear. It means acting in spite of your fear."*
>
> — Barbara De Angelis

Any time we are trying something new, going for a goal, or taking a risk, fear and negative self-talk seem to kick into overdrive.

Flash Point!
Here's a fact that we don't often think about:

Fear always accompanies growth.

If you're not a little bit afraid, you're probably not really growing.

So, when your negative self-talk starts in, ask yourself if it's just normal fear that develops when you are doing something you've never done before. Instead of viewing fear as a red light, or a stop sign, view fear as a green light! A sign that says, *"You're on the right track – you'll be OK, just keep going!"*

"Courage is doing what you're afraid to do. There can be no courage unless you're scared."
— Eddie Rickenbacker
(World War I fighter ace and Medal of Honor recipient.)

Fortes Fortuna Adiuvat. (Fortune favors the brave.)
— Terence

99% off course
If you've ever boarded an airline for a flight, you'll know that once you're airborne, the Captain often makes an announcement, and it goes something like this:

Ladies and gentlemen, this is your Captain speaking. We're headed for Los Angeles, California, and we will arrive at 4:28 p.m.

But while the plane is traveling to your destination, it is ***off course 99% of the time***. The autopilot (or on a rare occasion the actual pilot) is constantly correcting the plane and making adjustments as it travels off course. It banks to the right, it's corrected to the left – then it swerves too far, and is corrected again. This goes on for the whole trip.

When we're working toward a goal, there is a good chance that we'll be off-course 99% of the time, too. The result comes because we're traveling in the right general direction – we've taken action – and 1% success is good enough.

> *"If you go into the woods, expect mosquitoes. If you go after your goals, you can expect failure and mistakes."*
> — Brian Tracy

An Attitude of Gratitude

Don't forget in all of your haste to stop and be thankful for what you've achieved. Celebrate your achievements, no matter how great or small, with gratitude. Not only gratitude toward yourself, but also to those who help you along the way.

Don't be shy when it comes to thanking people that help you, inspire you, or make a difference in your life! Your gratitude might be just the thing that helps someone stretch that last bit toward their own goal.

> *"No matter what accomplishments you make, somebody helps you."*
> — Althea Gibson Darben

The Moral of the Story

Self-confidence and self-discipline are the best tools you can have in college. No one can control all of the circumstances life presents, but if you develop these tools, you can always rely on someone to carry you through the tough times – YOU!

Another thing to keep in mind is that it's hard to get what you want until you know what you want. To find true direction in your life, you need to become clear about the values and priorities that will shape your goals. Once you've done that and started down your path, there are no guarantees that it will be easy, but if you add a positive attitude to your self-confidence and self-discipline tools, there's very little that you can't find a way to overcome.

~

~ Chapter Four ~
Butcher, Baker or Candlestick Maker: College & Your Career

You might have thought we would have kept this chapter for the very end of the book. You work hard, you get through school, and then you look for a job, right? *Maybe not.*

We've put this topic here, toward the beginning of the book *not on a whim*, but for two solid reasons.

> **Reason number one:** Because we have two incredible tools online to help you explore career opportunities. They guide you through a process that gets you to think about what you really like, what type

> of environment you would work well in. Then it suggests jobs that would fit perfectly with you. When you discover a career you would love to have, it will guide the courses you take, it will give your time in college more of a sense of purpose, and it may shape what you do with your time off.
>
> **The second reason:** There are things you can start doing now to make your college degree worth even more. Things that will help you get better jobs, more pay, and increase your chances of loving what you do.

If you haven't done the Work Importance or Interest Profiler assessment online yet, hold off until you read this short chapter. We'll be giving you a lot of food for thought that will give you guidance when completing these assessments. If you have taken the assessments already, this chapter will help you clarify your most important considerations and direction.

To navigate, you need a direction

College is about different things to different people. For some, it's simply a requirement for their chosen career. For others, it's a chance to explore options and discover a direction. The sooner you have a direction, the more achievements related to your chosen career you can accumulate. This is why it's worth taking time to find one now.

Lack of direction is like being adrift at sea. Yes, you might get *somewhere* eventually, but is that the *somewhere* you really want to be? By leaving your life to chance you significantly lessen your chances of loving what you do. Sure, a lot of people don't take time to find their path in life, and they turn out ok. But are they really, truly satisfied and excited about what they're doing? The chances are much higher for you to be able to do *something you love* when you take time to find something you're excited about, and build your life from there.

My Time in College

Once upon a time I was in college, and I absolutely loved every minute of my time there. I knew from the time I was six years old that I wanted to be a Sports Injury Rehabilitation Specialist. I rushed through High School so that I could get to college where I would be free to pursue my dream! From my very first semester I studied physical therapy and learned so much about my dream career. I just couldn't believe how lucky I was that I would soon be working in this rewarding field.

Because I enjoyed each and every one of my classes so much, it was easy to study. I effortlessly got fantastic grades, and developed life-long relationships with my instructors.

Those weren't the only life-long relationships I made! My roommate became my best friend – we became the sisters each of us never had. Along with our close group of friends, we had the time of our lives. It seemed like every weekend, we enjoyed adventure and excitement.

In my third year, I met and fell in love with my husband, Rich. Rich majored in Sports Management and we have enjoyed working together throughout our whole careers. This coming year, we are going to retire together, buy a newer Lear Jet and travel for the next five years to explore our shared passion for the cultures of the world.

The End

Ok, answer honestly: Do you believe in this fairy tale? Many of us do. Isn't this the way it's supposed to work? Of course we're supposed to love every minute of college, right? We're supposed to be passionate and clear about what we want to do, too. We should be able to take career-oriented classes for our major during our very first semester, and the enjoyment of these classes should make it easy to study and get good grades.

We become best friends with our college roommate, and meet a group of friends that we love for life. Then we meet our spouse one day and fall madly in love. We never falter in our decision of what to do in our careers or our marriage, and we retire happily, with enough wealth to be comfortable and do whatever we want.

Holding your expectations this high can cause some problems. Of course there is no problem with aiming high and dreaming big. But when you expect your whole life to follow the fantasy script you've written, you can cause yourself stress when changes occur that don't fit in with your plan. That being said, read on, and don't give up on your dreams just yet.

Changing direction now, ever, or never

We realize that you may not feel comfortable making a decision about the direction your life is going to take right this very minute. Keep in mind that your direction can change, if at any time you decide you would rather pursue something else! It is perfectly acceptable to change your course in life, and more people are making more changes than ever these days.

So, although it may not be reasonable for you to know what you'll be doing twenty years from now, the best starting point for all of your possible careers is to get your degree. Aim to make a decision **for now**. Don't worry about if it is the right one for life. Just know that it is the right one... *for right now*!

"I might make the wrong choice!"

That's ok! If the idea of making the wrong choice is something that bothers you, keep in mind that everything that happens in your life gives you an opportunity to learn, and may even open up opportunities that you can't foresee. Life experiences change your perception of your world. You simply won't be the same person five years from now that you are today. Every single day brings with it the possibility of changing the way you see things. Of course your core values and personality type will be the same, but your priorities can and do change. Introducing an element of *"rolling with it"* in life leaves you room to live to your greatest potential.

Rolling with it doesn't mean remaining directionless until you're *"sure."* You may never be sure, and life **will** pass you by before you know it. Efforts that you make by choosing a direction, even if you change your mind, are never wasted. Effort is a part of the cycle of achievement. Without it, you can accomplish little and it's hard to remain motivated.

Flash Point!
Working toward your goal
In college, your purpose is pretty clear: get a degree. But you can refine that goal by choosing something to work toward that excites you. Goals that you have to meet but also want to meet are called self-concordant goals and they go a long way to making your life happier. Also, by being clear about your direction you can avoid working *away* from your goal – by doing things that may directly impede your progress. It happens!

Deciding on a major
You may already be clear about what you want to major in, and you may even be very passionate about it. If so, you'll already be familiar with some of the benefits of knowing what you want. If you haven't decided yet, this chapter along with the Interest Profiler and Work Importance assessments should really help you figure it out. Take some time to do a bit of soul-searching, too. When you've found the right major, it will **feel** right. It should be something that excites you, and something that you can clearly see yourself doing as a career.

Some powerful questions to journal on and mull over are:

1. **What are you really good at already?**
   Write everything down, even if it doesn't seem relevant or doesn't seem like something you could be paid to do.
2. **What do you really enjoy? What would you do for free?**
   Again, it doesn't matter if it seems like it can relate to a major for now.
3. **What is your dream work environment?**
   Do you like peace and quiet? Do you like to be surrounded, almost immersed in, what you are working on, with all of your work on the walls or desk to see? Or would you rather your work be tucked neatly away, out of view most of the time? Do you like to be out and about, or spend time in a room you consider to be **yours**? Are you a

people-person, or would you rather work alone? If you are a people-person, would you like to meet new people all the time, or stick to a group you know well?

The Work Importance Profiler will ask you similar questions to these, so it's a good idea to start thinking about them now. When you begin thinking about these types of questions, the real answers are not always instantly apparent, so sometimes the extra time can help a lot.

Difficulty deciding on a major

If you're having trouble choosing a major, or you have doubts about the one you chose, remember that what's most important is to get a *degree.*

The current average number of careers in a lifetime is between three and five, and going up. The best way to get started - no matter how many careers you're going to have - is to get started!

You might be surprised at what some people majored in:

~ Actress **Cate Blanchett** was an economics major, and so was **Tiger Woods.**

~ **David Letterman** majored in Telecommunications.

~ **Bruce Lee** majored in Philosophy.

~ Director **Wes Anderson** *(The Royal Tenenbaums, A Life Aquatic)* studied philosophy. While getting his degree, he met fellow student **Owen Wilson**, who received an English degree.

~ Actress **Mira Sorvino** graduated magna cum laude from Harvard with a degree in Asian Studies.

~ Bass player of KISS, **Gene Simmons**, majored in German.

~ Actor **Jake Gyllenhaal** majored in Eastern Religions.

~ Actor **Viggo Mortensen** majored in Government and Language.

Just because you choose a major doesn't mean you can't choose to do something different in your life.

Employers love focus and determination
Having a specific goal that you are excited about will compel you to do more extracurricular activities, try harder, and achieve more in school. All of these things look great to an employer, no matter what the subject.

Even if you've been working hard toward a goal and you change your mind, it doesn't alter the fact that you've exhibited an incredible amount of focus and determination to get as far as you did, which every employer values. You will almost certainly have learned some valuable things along the way, too. Focus and determination are also qualities you will need in abundance if you decide to start your own business.

> *"When I'm inspired, I get excited because I can't wait to see what I'll come up with next."*
> — Dolly Parton

Harvesting Skills
Getting specific about your goals helps you work toward them and it works the same way in college when you get specific about your major. Chances are that there will be hundreds, if not thousands of recent grads with your major going for the same jobs you will want when you graduate. What is going to set you apart? Employers don't simply hire the people who got the highest grades. They look for someone who will make a good employee. They'll look for a combination of skills and personality.

Sometimes referred to as *"soft skills"* and *"hard skills,"* the sooner you start to become aware of what your particular skills are, the more you can develop them.

Hard skills are things you can learn from a book, and are generally task-oriented. An example of this is excelling in computer programming, or proving yourself knowledgeable in your field. Being good with numbers is a hard skill, or public speaking if it might be required at your job.

Soft skills are generally people-oriented, and are a little harder to communicate to employers, so they will look for evidence of them in your resume and during your interview. Things like warmth, friendliness, ease in communication, drive, compassion or patience. Depending on the type of job you are going for, the right combination of soft skills may be just what the employer is searching for.

To try to determine your set of skills, the first thing a potential employer will do is search your resume for evidence. The more clearly you can communicate these skills, the more quickly your resume will be placed in the *"interview"* stack. To do this, you'll need to start collecting a few things:

~ **Get Involved**
Join clubs, organizations and teams while you're in college. They don't all have to be geared toward your major, but if they are, that's even better. The main benefits of getting involved are that you'll be presented with opportunities to gain new skills, face challenges and garner achievements. Oh, and you'll have fun meeting people, too!

~ **Collect Numbers**
Most people do a lot of explaining on their resume of what they have done, or can do. But not many can back this up with cold, hard data. How much did the fundraiser you were involved with earn? Was it more than the last year? If so, what percentage increase in earnings were you able to achieve? If you were an officer of a club or organization - or in any leadership position - how many members were involved at the time? Keep track. These will boost your resume and demand attention.

~ **Clock up achievement**
During an interview, or in your cover letter, it's best to be able to make reference to some specific achievements. So when you succeed, be sure to write it somewhere for later reference. Were any of your papers published? Did you have exceptional grades in a particular subject? Match the achievements you mention to the type of job you're looking for, and give the employer a good reason to hire you!

~ **Write down some challenges**
As you go through college, keep track of challenges you face, especially in a group situation. A popular interview question can be

something like, *"Tell us about a time when you were faced with a challenge, and explain how you overcame this obstacle."* Having a ready answer is impressive, especially when it pertains to a soft skill they might need.

~ **Log Initiative**
If you can show a potential employer that you are able to take initiative, you'll be a standout. Having initiative can be something as simple as making an extra effort on papers and reports. Maybe there is a professional you can interview to add weight to your final presentation or mid-term. If so, you can reference that as taking initiative. Showing initiative also impresses instructors, so you'll experience a double benefit for your efforts. In fact, you can show initiative even if you didn't succeed! Running for a student officer position - even if you weren't voted in - shows initiative.

~ **Start thinking like a…**
Whatever it is you want to do with your life, start to think like that now. If you can imagine yourself successfully working in this career, what might you look back and wish you had done differently in college? What can you do now that will add value to your career?

~ **Ask a professional**
Why not ask people working in your chosen career what they wish they had done in college? Ask them what they look for when hiring a new employee. Don't expect them to stop what they're doing to speak with you on the phone, but instead, ask the person on the phone for the professional's email address, so they can take their time and answer you when it's convenient. It can't hurt to ask, and you'll be surprised at how many people are willing to talk to someone who is making this effort. People who like what they do like to talk about it! And they often feel complimented by the fact that you sought them out.

Exercise

Brand: You. Knowing what you have to offer an employer.

Your time in college can also be seen as an opportunity to build a brand:

your own personal brand. Marketers often use the term *"Unique Selling Point"* or USP. This is how they explain what's so good about their business, and differentiate their businesses from the competition. To discover their USP, they begin by writing a company mission statement, exactly like the mission statement you created in Campus ToolKit (or will soon create).

Then they use their mission statement to create a tagline. A tagline is a highly condensed mission statement or a line that conveys the feeling or vision of an organization.

What makes a good tagline? Here are a few highly successful taglines from top companies:

~ Think Different. *(Apple)*

~ Don't leave home without it. *(American Express)*

~ Melts in your mouth, not in your hands. *(M&M's)*

As a potential employee, you will have a USP too. Skills that you have harvested are a big part of developing a unique angle that only ***you*** can offer. Once you know what you can bring to the job, you'll need to find a way to verbalize it, either on you résumé, in your cover letter, or during your interview. A great exercise to hone your USP is to create a tagline from your mission statement. Then put it someplace where you can see it often to start building your brand. Nike did it. Just do it!

We've given you some space here to work on a tagline. If you haven't completed your mission statement, it might be helpful to do that first. We've got a special tool online to help.

Tagline:

____

____

____

More than a career

Ever notice how some people have more than a just a job – they have a career?

Some people take it a step further, and they somehow have even more than a career. They seem to be so at one with what they're doing that it becomes an extension of who they are. You can almost guarantee that even if they no longer needed an income, they would still get up and do the exact same thing every day. Maybe Madonna. Maybe Tiger Woods. Oprah Winfrey, Cameron Diaz, Bill Gates and Steve Jobs. Maybe someone you know personally. When people have more than a career, their successes seem effortless. Of course they face the same challenges as everyone else, but their love for what they're doing carries them through. They are motivated by passion.

Is there any reason why you shouldn't have more than a career? If this appeals to you, you can absolutely have it. It starts by discovering your direction in life. So NOW is probably a good time to take our online Work Importance and Interest Profiler assessments. Do some journaling and spend time thinking carefully about what you really want, and who you really are. Start investing in yourself now, and you'll be rewarded with more than a career. You'll be living with passion!

Flash Point!
Be happy now
Don't forget to enjoy your time now. College is a time of preparation for the future, but it's important to live in the moment and enjoy every day while you're here. After all, even after graduation there will always be something you're aiming for. You'll always have goals, but by their very nature goals are future-oriented. Don't get SO focused on the future that you stop enjoying what you are doing as you pursue those goals.

"If I wait to be happy, I'll wait forever. If I'm happy now, I'll be happy forever."
— Anonymous

Assessments

Career Interest Profiler

This assessment is designed to help you discover your vocational interests. Put simply, it's about knowing what you're really going to like in a job, and avoiding work that you'll dislike. Sometimes the idea of a career can sound really fun. For example, when you think of being a florist, what comes to mind?

Friendly exchanges with happy customers? Ordering beautiful flowers and creating artful arrangements? Being surrounded by vivid colors?

What about the constant cleaning of flower bins to avoid the spread of disease and molds? Being in the same place, day after day? Working most weekends and holidays? Dealing with angry brides who ordered *blush* ribbons, not *mauve*, and thus your mistake has ruined their whole wedding?

We can't always anticipate the downsides - or the upsides to all careers. This assessment will help you by measuring your occupational interests, and matching them to a database of over 900 jobs.

The Interest Profiler measures six types of occupational interests:

1. Realistic
2. Investigative
3. Artistic
4. Social
5. Enterprising
6. Conventional

It then ranks these categories according to the answers you provide, and gives you an opportunity to experiment with your various interests and explore potential careers.

Work Importance Profiler

This career exploration tool helps you to focus on what qualities are important to you in a job. It then identifies occupations that you may find satisfying, based on the similarity between your work values and the characteristics of the occupations.

The Work Importance Profiler measures six types of work values:

1. Achievement
2. Independence
3. Recognition
4. Relationships
5. Support
6. Working Conditions

Then, like the Career Interest Profiler, it will rank these categories and let you experiment with these aspects and explore potential careers.

When you're finished taking these assessments, you can save careers you might be interested in from the database, or print them. Take your time with these, since your chosen career will shape your choice of a major, and you'll want to pick something you'll really enjoy and be truly satisfied with. However, if you feel you just can't decide – just pick your top choice for now. As you work through this book, your decision may become clearer to you.

The Moral of the Story

What would you really, really love to do for a living? College is the perfect place to dream up a rewarding career. Sometimes it's hard to make a decision - it can be difficult to narrow a whole world of choices down! That's why we've given you two assessments that consider who you are, and then suggest careers that could work for you. But relax. Choosing a career isn't a life sentence – it's estimated that many of us will enjoy several careers in our lifetime. By avoiding a decision you evade your own future, but making a decision allows you to start gathering skills for an impressive résumé. Don't worry about the possibility that you will change your mind – efforts you have made, no matter what the subject – will look great to a future employer.

~ Chapter Five ~
Don't wait for Midnight: Time Management

"You will never 'find' time for anything. If you want time you must make it."
— Charles Buxton

If you are attending college directly from high school, you'll find that college places very different demands on your time. At first glance, it may appear that you'll have even more free time than ever, because you may have less actual class time. But beware – college usually requires a lot more study time than you needed in high school. This freedom and lack of structure can really tax your time management skills.

If you're a returning student, you are probably juggling a job and maybe a family. Now that you're adding the time needed to commute to campus, attend classes and do homework, it can get overwhelming in a hurry.

Here's the deal with time management: most of us don't *think* about it until we've hit a snag, or hit the wall, or have just plain run out of time. This usually happens during exam week, or when we have a big assignment or paper due, or when we get sick and fall behind. By then, we're so pressed for time that we feel we don't *have time* to dedicate to constructing a plan.

The funny thing is, when the crunch period passes, we go back to having *"all the time in the world"* and we still don't develop a time management plan.

No matter where you are in this cycle, you will always benefit from making the time to get organized, and create a time management plan ... and Campus ToolKit can help!

What is Time Management?
Time management is everything that helps you plan for and effectively:

~ Set aside enough time to study

~ Avoid having to cram for tests

~ Keep up-to-date with assignments

~ Overcome procrastination

~ Balance study time and personal time

~ Create a study schedule and stick to it

Time management is not just about carefully documenting your time and commitments and then following a strict routine. It's not about making you a perfectly efficient person (or robot) either. The point of time management is that when you are good at it, your life and your successes get easier.

Flash Point!
Studies have shown that time management has the strongest correlation with a student's overall success in a course. In other words, the more you manage your time, the better your chances of getting good grades.

What happens when you *don't* have a plan?
You can miss important assignments, turn in work late, and get behind in your studies. This leads to cramming for tests and brings on a lot of unnecessary pressure. It causes anxiety. It makes you feel frustrated with yourself and with school. It can even create feelings of guilt and disappointment – especially when you're procrastinating.

Why should you care about time management?
If you haven't found yourself in a time pinch yet, it's inevitable that it will happen at some point if you're not practicing time management principles. When this happens, your stress levels skyrocket, your grades can suffer, and your career success can be jeopardized.

A huge benefit of time management is that it helps you identify activities that *waste your time*, giving you back more free time to do whatever you want.

The thing about time management is that it isn't hard to do, and it doesn't take long to implement on a daily basis. All it takes is an initial investment to discover how you spend your time now, and a plan for how you can better spend your time for success.

Let's get to it! We've created a system of online, personalized tools you can use to get on top of time management. We'll guide you through each one, so it's best if you can be in front of your computer for the first part of this chapter.

Awareness
How are you currently spending your time? How much study time do you have available on a daily basis?

Try our Daily Time Tracker exercise in your online tools to see how you are typically spending your day. Print the results of the exercise if you can.

How did you do? Can you see where this schedule might change during the weeks leading up to an exam? Each semester, your schedule will change depending on your course load, extracurricular activities, and work schedule. Later in this chapter we'll give you guidelines on how much time to spend studying.

When Time Management Fails

Before you start on your time management plan, there are a few pitfalls to avoid.

Inflexibility

It's tempting to plan your time to the minute, or prepare a daily schedule and apply it to the entire semester. Ideally, this should work, but in reality it never does. A flexible schedule is more likely to work in the *"real world."*

Starting when you're behind

If you are designing your time management plan in response to falling behind, you're most likely going to have to place heavy time expectations on yourself in order to catch up. Remember that this is only temporary – so be sure to revisit your new plan after the pressure has eased to make adjustments, and add more preparation time to avoid falling behind in the future.

Creating the *"ideal"* plan - that doesn't work for YOU?!

Your time management plan has to work with your personality. A plan that works well for one student might be impossible for another.

If you haven't already, now is a great time to complete some of the assessments available to you on Campus ToolKit. Knowing your personality type (DISC), taking a quick Visual, Auditory, Tactile and Kinesthetic learning style assessment (Sensory Learning Styles), and taking the Paragon Learning Style Inventory (PLSI) gives you a tremendous advantage when it comes to creating a time management plan that works for you.

Rather than trying to change your personality to manage your time a certain way, you're better off managing your time in a way that works with your personality and learning style.

Taking control of your time

When it comes to your schedule, it's important to remember that **you** are the one who is in control. Think of your schedule as a tool that guides you, and not as a law that has to be abided by. Flexibility is key to time management, and how much flexibility you want is up to you!

A good way to look at your schedule is like a time map, with all of your commitments clearly laid out in front of you. How you get to them is your choice.

Part of taking control is taking responsibility for your time, and accepting that you may have to change some of your habits and behaviors. After you've completed your time schedule, we'll give you tips to help you form new habits.

Know yourself!

Time Management is very personal, and you can personalize the way your schedule works. If you enjoy making lists and ticking off completed tasks, you might like a more rigid time schedule to give you a sense of accomplishment. If you prefer to leave your possibilities open, you might want a less rigid schedule - maybe just a to-do list to keep you on track. Make sure that however you design your schedule, you check frequently to make sure it's working **for** you, and not causing frustration!

Estimating your time

You've already done a broad estimation of how you spend a typical day. Now, let's get a little more detailed by estimating the time you are currently spending per week on activities and commitments. We've developed an interactive weekly schedule to help you estimate, which can be found online in your tools. When you're finished, print or save the results.

Tracking time

Now that you have estimated your time, it's important to actually track your time for the next week to see how your estimate compares to your actual time spent. Tracking your time is important if you sometimes wonder where time has gone. It also helps when determining whether you generally under or over-estimate the time needed to complete a task.

For the next week, keep a log of your time on an hourly basis. When you're finished, you'll use this information to adjust your new schedule. If you'd like to print this out, you can find the weekly time tracker PDF under the Tools > Exercises menu online.

Weekly Time Tracker

	SUN	MON	TUES	WED	THUR	FRI	SAT
6:00 AM							
7:00 AM							
8:00 AM							
9:00 AM							
10:00 AM							
11:00 AM							
12:00 PM							
1:00 PM							
2:00 PM							
3:00 PM							
4:00 PM							
5:00 PM							
6:00 PM							
7:00 PM							
8:00 PM							
9:00 PM							
10:00 PM							
11:00 PM							
12:00 PM							
1:00 AM							

Over-Estimators and Under-Estimators

Most of us can't predict with total accuracy how much time something is going to take. We can, however, learn our own tendencies and budget our time accordingly.

Under-Estimators

If you find that you continually under-estimate the amount of time a job will take, then you need to learn to add time to your estimates.

Some people are optimists by nature, and tend to think things will be easier or take less time than they do. If that's you, learn how much time you are really spending on tasks by logging your time. When you see these actual figures, re-arrange your schedule accordingly.

> **Flash Point!**
> When estimating time for new tasks, assignments, or courses, decide how much time you think they will take, and double it! This doubled figure is usually far closer to the actual figure than your first optimistic guess.

If you double the amount of time you think tasks will take, you may schedule more time than you actually need. However, while you are learning better time management, this is important so that you'll avoid getting frustrated or behind in your schedule. Once you get a better feel for the amount of time the task actually takes, you can change your schedule to reflect that time.

Over-Estimators

When you track the actual time you spend on tasks, you may find that you over-estimated the time you needed to finish. This often happens if you don't focus your attention completely on the task at hand.

For example, let's say you estimate that it takes two hours to complete your math homework. However, when you track your *actual* activities, you might discover that you spent twenty minutes eating snacks, and that you read and responded to twenty five instant messages that took sixty seconds each.

Instead, if you were to bring a snack to your desk, and close your messaging programs while you studied, you could have an extra forty-five minutes of free time in your day! Math homework would feel a lot less time consuming, and you could have real interaction with someone instead of half-math, half-messages.

How much time should I spend?

Here is a guideline to how much time you can expect to spend on schoolwork. This is only a guideline, because every one has a different schedule, and you will have to budget your time in a way that works for **your unique lifestyle**.

Schoolwork

Plan to spend two to three hours per week for every academic credit. That means if you have a full schedule of fifteen credits, you can expect to spend thirty to forty-five hours doing homework and studying every week!

For easy classes, you may find that two hours per week, per credit is enough.

For average classes, three hours a week, per credit may be needed.

For very difficult classes, you may need up to four hours per week, per credit. However, needing up to four hours per week can be a sign of ineffective study methods. Simply monitor your activities, and make sure you're not wasting time. Only you can decide how much time you need for each class.

Calculate your study time for this semester here, or go online and use our automated calculator under the tools menu.

Study Time

Easy class credits		*x 2 hrs, =*	*hrs.*
Average class credits		*x 3 hrs. =*	*hrs.*
Difficult class credits		*x 4 hrs. =*	*hrs.*
		Total study time per week:	***hrs.***

Leisure Time

Taking 10% of your week, or seventeen hours, during college is a good guideline for leisure time. Leisure time is time to relax, plan, read, exercise, and have fun, so be sure to schedule it in!

Flash Point!
Expecting the Unexpected

Allow time in your schedule for unexpected events, like getting sick, doctors' appointments, social functions and dream dates! This is where an inflexible schedule fails. Life always throws something unexpected at you, so be sure you have room in your schedule to handle it.

Making To-Do Lists

To-do lists are at the very core of any time management system. Along with a schedule, they are a daily reminder of chores, errands, and items you need to remember to do.

Writing something on your to-do list should be viewed as a commitment, or a promise to yourself that you will complete the task.

In general, when you finish a job, draw a line through it. If you don't get to finish that day, draw an arrow forward, and transfer the job to your to-do list the next day. If you've cancelled a job, cross it out with an "*x*," or place an "*x*" beside it.

The most important to-do list you will make is a daily to-do list. Following that, a weekly to-do list can be handy for an overview. You can make daily, hourly, weekly, monthly, or per-semester to-do lists.

A to-do list can take almost any form, from fancy planners to a piece of paper stuck to the wall. Here are some popular methods:

3x5 Cards

For each day, create a 3x5 card with all your tasks to be completed that day. For every job you finish, draw a line through it and move on to the next job. Keep the card in your pocket or backpack where you can reference it quickly, making sure you're not forgetting something.

A small notebook
This can also serve as a daily to-do list. Just write the date at the top and start a new to-do list on the next page for each day. An advantage of using this method is that you can look back easily on previous days to see when you completed a task.

Using a planner
Planners are tools designed to make time management easier. They often come with a monthly schedule section, so that you can schedule and view upcoming events at a glance, as well as space for daily to-do lists. They come in all shapes and sizes, so choose one that is convenient and fits easily in your backpack or handbag.

A big advantage of a planner is that you always have both your schedule and to-do lists with you, in one place. If you need to make a note of something, it goes in the planner, so that you eliminate scraps of paper (and the common problem of losing them) from your life.

Campus ToolKit To-Do List
You have a very handy to-do list available to you online in Campus ToolKit. Keep all your to-do items here and there is no risk of losing them.

Campus ToolKit Reminders
When something is coming up that you just can't risk forgetting, add it to the Reminder tool online. Campus ToolKit will automatically send you an email to jog your memory. You tell us when you want to be reminded, and rest assured we'll remind you when you log on that day. Be sure you're logging onto the system regularly for this feature to be effective.

Other fancy gadgets
Many mail programs, like Microsoft Outlook, have built-in calendars. You can also buy electronic planners. Some of these can double as your phone, and allow you to check emails. Use whatever planner appeals to you most!

Scheduling
Just like to-do lists, scheduling is at the heart of any time management system. A great time to fill in your schedule is Sunday night, before your school week starts.

Begin by scheduling the time you need for sleep. Most people need seven to nine hours of sleep every night. Getting up earlier than normal affects your concentration even more than going to bed later than normal, so aim to wake up at the same time every day if possible.

A word of caution: Many students use their sleep time as a cushion for poor time management, losing sleep when they get behind on their studies. This is a bad practice, because losing sleep affects your concentration levels, ability to focus, and increases the likelihood of anxiety and making mistakes. You will never get the opportunity to be at your best during any given day by doing this. Make sleep a priority!

Next, schedule in all of your fixed commitments that you are required to meet, like class times, job hours, and organization meetings. Use your class syllabus to layout assignments and exams for the semester.

Then, create an intermediate schedule. This should be done once a week, and includes the work to be completed in each subject week-by-week in order to stay current in all your classes. It also includes events that are happening during the week. For example:

__ Complete Outline for English Paper

__ History Quiz Wednesday

__ Read 50 pages in Sociology by Friday

__ Swimming Tuesday afternoon

__ Movies Saturday night!

Transfer to your daily to-do lists from here.

These are popular methods for scheduling:

Notebook – Cheap and Cheerful
This is very much like the notebook used for to-do lists. Simply put the date at the top of each page. The only thing you will have to add is a month-at-a-glance section, which you can make. You can also print out the calendar in Campus ToolKit and use that for your month-at-a-glance.

Planners
Planners provide a convenient place to organize schedules and to-do lists, as well as other important information. They usually come with a month-at-a-glance section, which is handy for scheduling fixed commitments. Time is usually broken into either daily or weekly compartments after that. Some days are split into to-do lists and diaries for keeping track of your daily activities.

Planners also offer other features, like a place to keep contacts, reference materials, and sometimes goal and project sheets. Shop around and find a planner that has what you need, and fits in your backpack or handbag.

Although planners provide very sophisticated time management assistance, they are expensive. They also take a certain amount of regular commitment to use – remember, you can't buy time management just by buying a fancy planner. Consider carefully before you invest; in many cases a simple pen and paper to-do list, or the Campus ToolKit calendar will work just as well, and they're free!

Campus ToolKit Calendar Feature
Campus ToolKit features an easy-to-use calendar that lets you schedule and view your activities, or create a printed calendar to hang on your bulletin board. If you work on your computer daily, the Campus ToolKit time management tools (to-do lists, reminders, and calendar) might be the easiest option for you.

Scheduling for big projects
When you have a large project to work on, like a term paper, thesis, or oral report, the job gets a lot easier to handle when you break the tasks into small segments, with individual timelines for each section. Take a look at your class syllabus for each course, and start planning larger projects now, before they sneak up on you.

Don't forget to schedule your small segments, or use the Campus ToolKit reminder feature to prompt you to start when it's time.

Monitoring your time
Part of time management is checking your schedule against reality, similarly to how you did at the beginning of this module. This is how you'll know when it's time to make changes to your schedule.

For example, if you scheduled two hours of study for your sociology class, keep an eye on that. Is it enough to keep current? Or do you find that you're falling behind? Also, consider whether two hours is still going to be enough before a test or exam. Remember to schedule in *flexibility* and not perfectionism!

Prioritizing
Once you have organized your tasks, and have a to-do list, it's important that you schedule your priorities first. This is how you can see *at a glance* which projects to work on first, and which projects can be put on hold.

It's a natural human tendency to do the easiest, or most fun task first. If you have an English term paper due at the end of the week, and an exciting art project due at the end of the month, make sure your English paper has priority over the fun art assignment.

There are many ways of prioritizing your tasks. Some are simple, and others are more philosophical. The simple methods work well for prioritizing daily to-do lists. For scheduling, taking a wider view will help you feel more enthusiastic about what you are doing. You'll feel more motivated when you have a clear understanding of *why* priorities are prioritized.

Here are a few methods of prioritizing - choose whichever works for you!

Numbering your tasks

After making a to-do list, number each task in order of importance. That means that if working on your English exam is number one, and arranging a ball game for Thursday night is number five, you stick to that order, getting your priorities out of the way first.

The A-B-C Method

When scheduling jobs and tasks, label them according to their importance and urgency.

A. Tasks are the most important, most urgent, highest priority.

C. Tasks are the least important, least urgent, lowest priority.

B. Tasks are in between.

When you work down your lists of tasks, you start with A Tasks and work down to C Tasks.

Big Rocks First

Steven Covey, in his book *"First Things First"* tells a story one of his associates heard at a seminar:

> Imagine taking a wide mouth gallon jar and filling it with fist-sized rocks - all the way to the top of the jar - until absolutely no more rocks will fit in.
>
> Is the jar full?
>
> Then take pebbles, and add them to the jar, jiggling the jar until the pebbles fill all the spaces between the rocks. Is the jar full now?
>
> Add some sand, shaking the jar, and scooping in more, until the jar is filled to the very top. Now is it full?
>
> Pour in water until the water reaches the very brim of the jar.
> Now, the jar is full.

It might seem that the point of this illustration is that you can always fit more things into your life *"if you really work at it,"* and this is how many students operate their time.

Instead, the point is: if you don't put the big rocks in first, you would never have gotten any of them in. Try filling the jar first with sand. Can you fit any pebbles in? If the jar was filled with water first, could you fit any big rocks in?

As you schedule and prioritize your tasks, think of the *"big rocks"* in your life as the things you do that are in line with your values and goals. These are things that make you happier, more fulfilled, and healthier. For example, getting grades that are good enough to allow you to go to law school, and realize your dream career. Or exercising, eating and sleeping enough to be at your best and feel well.

The pebbles represent the things we like to do – things that make life enjoyable, like a ball game on the weekend or a movie night with friends.

We all have things we have to do, like pay bills and do the dishes, which is like the sand.

And then we have the water: anything that gets everywhere and clutters your life. Water can be anything from instant messaging and phone calls to worries and stress. This *"water"* is inevitable, and we all have it in our lives.

The trick is to start with the big rocks, and fill your jar (that's your schedule, dig?) based on your priorities.

The A-B does it work *for me* method
This A-B method is very simple and will appeal to you if you have very clear, specific goals in your life:

A. Activities bring you closer to your goals and priorities.

B. Activities take you further from your goals and priorities.

If you haven't already, now is a great time to complete the mission statement exercise online. This helps you zero-in on your priorities in life. Choosing your priorities is the cornerstone to having a fulfilling life that is full of purpose.

Now, let's say you've completed a **mission statement** that says your purpose is to bring happiness and joy to the people in your life. You also have a **goal** to graduate with honors so that you can attend the law school of your choice. You'll need law school because you have a **dream** of being the District Attorney of the City of San Francisco.

As you fill your schedule, and as you go about your day, ask yourself, *"Is this an A activity that gets me closer to my goal, or a B activity?"* If it's an A activity, proceed, or schedule it. If it's a B activity, dump it.

> **For example:**
> If it's a Sunday afternoon and you're up-to-date with your homework and studying, going to the movies with friends might be an A activity. It relaxes you, and gives you time to enjoy life and feel centered.
>
> However, if you have scheduled two hours of study this afternoon for a history exam, going to the movies would be a B activity – taking you further from your goal of good grades and a rewarding career.
>
> Even though the movie would be just as relaxing and enjoyable, the end result would leave you unprepared for your exam, or stressed and cramming instead of on-schedule and feeling good.

Running out of time
If your schedule is working pretty well, but you find you are still not getting everything done, try a few of these tips before you make any drastic changes.

Learning to say "No."

> *"I don't know the key to success, but the key to failure is trying to please everybody."*
> — Bill Cosby

It's hard to say no. We all like to feel needed, and approved, and one way we do this is by doing things for other people. This makes it hard to say no when somebody wants something. You may not really want to do what they're asking, but you don't want to hurt the person's feelings or offend them – or more importantly, let them down.

The main problem with not saying no is that you often sacrifice your own needs. Learning to say no with confidence helps you stay on track with your goals. Saying no is about respecting yourself.

An easy way to say no is to acknowledge the other person's feelings first, and then explain your feelings or reasons. For example, *"I know you've got the whole day off Saturday, and I would love to be able to have a nice lunch with you; but I have a big test coming up, and I have scheduled that time to study. This class is really important to me, and I want a good grade."*

If they persist (or beg) just hold your ground, saying *"I'm terribly sorry, I just can't."*

The oldest trick in the book
Add an extra hour to your day. If you are a morning person, get up an hour earlier. If you are productive at night, work an extra hour or two then.

Work during peak energy times
Pay attention to when you are at your best. If you are tired or drowsy in the afternoon, reading the same amount of pages or studying at that time could take twice as long as it would during a time when you are naturally alert and focused.

Stay focused
When you're short on time, completely focus on the task at hand.
That means that if you're studying, you study. You're not doing laundry, or making snacks, or instant messaging, or walking the dog, or watching a bit of TV. *You're just studying*. When you're finished, that's the time to do all your other chores and fun stuff.

Set goals
Decide how many pages you are going to read, write it down, and stick to it. Use our assignment job list to break large projects into smaller steps. Having goals, even small ones, helps you stay focused and on track.

Using down-time and spare minutes
We all do a lot of waiting. We wait in lines, wait for class to start, wait for

our meal or coffee at a café, and wait for the bus or train. You can turn your waiting time into productive time by reviewing notes, studying note cards or flash cards, and reading while you wait.

By finishing small tasks during these spare minutes, you'll have more time to focus on the bigger tasks.

Commuting time is another opportunity. While on the train or bus, catch up on reading. If you drive, record your lectures and listen back for key points.

> *"Much may be done in those little shreds and patches of time, which every day produces and which most men throw away."*
> — Proverb

Take time to get organized
Although getting organized takes time, it is time well spent. No matter how good your schedule is, you can lose hours every week by wasting time looking for misplaced keys, textbooks, papers, bills, notes, handouts and backpacks.

More Time-Savers
Here are some more tips to organize your time:

Flash Point!
Turn off your phone and close your IM and email programs when you need to get something done
Constant interruptions waste more time than they actually take. Every time you are interrupted, it takes a moment or two to get back into what you are doing. Instant messaging, surfing the net and reading or writing emails are insidious, and they will end up wasting a lot of your time in ways that are hard to predict, and difficult to put your finger on.

OHIO – Only Handle It Once
We spend a lot of time looking through papers, sorting and re-sorting things. Instead of allowing this time-wasting activity, you can choose to only handle it once.

For example:
Upon receiving a big stack of mail, you might shuffle through, pulling out a few letters that interest you, and put the pile down again to deal with another time. Later, when you need to pay your Visa bill, you shuffle through again to find that.

Instead, sort the stack only once, making piles of items to read now, placing all bills in one pile to pay together at one time, and throwing junk mail directly into the trash can.

Be selective and protective
Every day we are bombarded with thousands of marketing messages, hundreds of television viewing and reading opportunities, and dozens of opportunities to have a chat with someone. When it comes to information, it pays to select only information that will actually be of use to you. If time is tight, which it is for most college students, then you have to protect your time and your schedule from these unwanted intrusions.

Use technology to your advantage
Utilize online banking services, get your paycheck by direct deposit, send an instant message instead of having a conversation, and order your prescription refills from online pharmacies. All of these technologies can save valuable time.

Creating New Habits
Just like learning anything new, getting good at time management takes practice. The more you work at it, the better you'll get. Eventually, you won't have to think so hard about how to use time effectively - your behaviors will become habits.

Creating new habits starts with awareness of behaviors that aren't working for you. That's why you estimated your time first - to see if you're an under-estimator or an over-estimator. Next you tracked your time - to discover where you might be wasting time.

Once you know what your habits are, you can set out to create new ones with clarity. But don't expect to change overnight! Changing habits takes time, and trying to force change too quickly will usually cause failure.

Homer Simpson puts it well when he says, *"Going cold turkey isn't as delicious as it sounds."*

Overcoming internal barriers

Changing habits can be especially challenging because there are all sorts of barriers, both internal and external, that tend to nudge you back to your old way of doing things. The following is a short list of ways to overcome internal barriers:

> **Ask for help**
>
> When you're having trouble, don't forget to reach out, or ask for help from those who know you best. You're surrounded with thousands of people who are trying just as hard as you to balance time pressures – so ask for help!
>
> You can also ask for help with a specific problem, like an assignment, or a distraction. Your instructor or teaching assistant is available during office hours to help. If you have a problem with a distraction, ask other students what they do. If a specific person is the problem, ask for his or her help to decrease the distraction.
>
> For example, if your roommate makes too much noise at night and you lose sleep because of it, ask for help with the problem. If you approach the situation with an open mind, a solution can be found.
>
> **Anxiety about time**
>
> *"Our main business is not to see what lies dimly at a distance, but to do what lies clearly at hand."*
>
> — Thomas Carlyle
>
> If you find yourself worrying about your schedule or getting everything done, think of to-do lists and schedules as tools to help you remember, so that you don't have to worry so much. They help get things **out** of your head, so that you have one place to look at your

schedule instead of trying to remember. It also saves worry about double-booking and forgetting.

Start with right now, and don't think beyond it. Focus on what you'll do **this day** to achieve your goals. Don't stress yourself about tomorrow or next week. Just ask yourself what you can do today, right now, to work toward your goals … and that's what will go on your to-do list.

By narrowing your focus to the present or the very near-term future, your time pressures often seem far less daunting. Once you start listing EVERYTHING you have to do over the next week or even the next month, it's easy to get a little freaked out. Just take a moment, get organized for today, and get started. You'll start to check things off your list and that will give you the satisfaction of seeing progress.

Taking breaks and burning out

Nobody can work all of the time - your mind needs rest and relaxation. When you don't take time out, and you get tired, tasks take longer to complete and you are more likely to make mistakes.

You're also going to find yourself short of ideas, both creatively and strategically. It's during your quiet time, or your fun interaction with other people that you'll get your best ideas.

We tend to burn out especially during times when we're behind. Burning out means you have not taken time to refuel. The only way to avoid burnout is to schedule your time so that you have time to recharge and reinvigorate yourself.

Getting Sick

Your body will take care of itself, and that includes getting sick if you are not taking good care of yourself. Why? It's your body's way of saying, *"Hey, if you're not going to take a break, I'll make you take a break!"*

Unfortunately, these breaks can't be scheduled and tend to come at very inconvenient times – like during exam week, or during your long-overdue holiday! It's a lot more efficient - and a whole lot more comfortable - to plan for the relaxation we just talked about so that you stay healthy.

Procrastination

"The road to success is paved with the most tempting parking places."
— Anonymous

What it is

Procrastination is the most common downfall to any time management program. All the scheduling advice in the world cannot compete with procrastination. Interestingly, procrastination has very little to do with time management. Think about it: when you're procrastinating, you know exactly what you *should* be doing – *you're just not doing it*!

Everyone experiences procrastination to one degree or another. For some, it's a minor problem – something that causes us inconvenience at times. For others, it's a constant problem that causes lots of stress and anxiety.

Procrastination is sometimes borne out of optimism, when you are overly optimistic about the amount of time something is going to take.

Let's say you've been given an assignment for a term paper that you estimate will take six days to complete. You have three weeks until the project is due, so that's plenty of time. You may even decide to *"beat"* procrastination this time and schedule the work well in advance…

…BUT, you know that you've got extra time, and you don't *really* have to start yet. So you put it off, borrowing time from next week, or tomorrow, again and again.

Suddenly, you realize you are out of time and you need to start. Instead of feeling relaxed, you are now feeling stressed and under pressure.

When you actually begin the work, you often realize that it is going to take more time than you thought. This produces feelings of fear and panic. You might get a bad grade! You might not finish it in time, and it's important!

Eventually you concede that you'll have to rush the project. This leads to feelings of guilt and disappointment in yourself, but you get it done and turn it in on-time.

Here's where it gets interesting: You may even manage to get a decent grade. This gives you a mixed bag of feelings – pride that you finished and did a good job – but only partially. You also feel guilt that you may have received an undeserved grade, or even disdain for the instructor who couldn't spot a rush job.

The main lesson you end up learning from this episode is that you received positive reinforcement for procrastinating. In other words, you pulled it off.

Why you do it

We like to tell ourselves that we are in control, and that we are *choosing* to put off the project. We can start any time, and things will be fine. But the fact is that we often have negative feelings about the task that we don't readily want to see or admit to. If you have negative feelings, you will always tend to put off or delay.

Here are some common reasons for procrastination and negative feelings:

~ **The project seems too big**. When things are too big, we don't know where to start – so we don't! We also feel overwhelmed because the project requires large blocks of time, which aren't always available.

  The truth is that large blocks of time are hardly ever available. However, it's better to start small than not start at all. If you're feeling unsure about where to start, try mind mapping or creating an outline. This is often just enough to get you over that *"too big"* feeling.

~ **Fear of Failure**. The safest way not to fail is not to try. Nobody wants to make mistakes, so we often feel afraid to start a new project for fear of being wrong.

  Reassure yourself that you can figure it out – that you can handle it! Try listing the reasons you think the project might not work

– usually this highlights the silliness of any further delay. If you identify real concerns, address them one by one looking for solutions. If you can't solve the issues yourself, ask for help!

~ **Perfectionism**. When you put undue pressures on yourself to be perfect, it can make a new task overwhelming.

  Often, just getting a start alleviates these tendencies. No one expects you to be perfect – even your instructors! What's most important to them is that you have gained an understanding of the material.

~ **Difficult or unpleasant tasks**. When something is difficult or we don't like the task, we will always tend to put it off.

  Tell yourself it won't be that bad, and remind yourself that you can play when your work is finished.

~ **Simple habit**. Sometimes procrastination is just a behavioral habit you are in. This happens when you respond to what is urgent, or to what seems easiest, instead of what is really important.

What you tell yourself

A common excuse procrastinators use to justify their delay tactics is, *"I work better under pressure."* Guess what? You don't! The reason you work *"better"* under pressure is because you have no choice. Your back is against the wall, and you simply must perform. You would have been able to work just as well whenever you chose to act, even if that was three weeks ago. In fact, you probably perform better when you are not under pressure – you just don't know it because you never give yourself the chance.

You might also recognize these gems:

~ I'll do it tomorrow

~ I'll do it tomorrow, if…

~ I've been working hard – I deserve some fun first

~ I just need to clear my mind before I get started

~ I'm in the wrong major – I would enjoy something else more

~ I'm in the wrong school – this one doesn't work for me

~ I'll just read this first, and then I'll get going…

~ Right after this TV program

Paying the price

What you rob yourself of when you procrastinate is your freedom. You lose the feeling of being in control of your life.

The other problem is that your time is not your own when you are procrastinating. Yes, you may be at a barbecue enjoying good company, but in the back of your mind, you know you're *really* supposed to be doing something else. When you get into a pattern, or habit, of procrastinating, you may start to feel like your time is never your own - you're always behind - you should always be doing *"something else."*

In fact, when procrastination becomes a habit, you really are always behind. When you finally finish a project, you can be so wasted by all the effort it took that you need a break. When the break is finished, you're already behind on your next project. And so it continues.

Other costs of procrastination are stress, anxiety, feeling helpless and feeling useless or undeserving.

Changing the Procrastination habit

Step 1: ACTION!

> *"Inaction breeds doubt and fear. Action breeds confidence and courage. If you want to conquer fear, do not sit home and think about it. Go out and get busy."*
>
> — Dale Carnegie

Flash Point!

All of the great ideas in the world can't beat an average idea that is acted upon. When you're having trouble getting started on a goal, start moving. Find a way to do something...*anything* toward your goal. Action kills procrastination.

Make a plan

This is often all it takes when something seems too big, too difficult, or when you're feeling paralyzed by perfection. A plan doesn't need to be complex - it can be a simple mind map, or a quick list of steps. This is effective because it requires you to take action. Making a plan gets you going, and gives you direction.

The Ten-Minute Rule

When you are having difficulty getting started on something, just commit to working only ten minutes. Usually, this is enough to get interested and get going on the project.

Decide to change

When faced with a time challenge, it's helpful to stop and ask yourself, *"What would my normal behavior be?"* Then, consciously decide to choose a better option.

Enthusiasm

Enthusiasm is like a secret key to motivate you and abolish procrastination. When you feel enthused about something, you naturally *want* to do it.

Enthusiasm is part of the Higher Achievement Cycle:

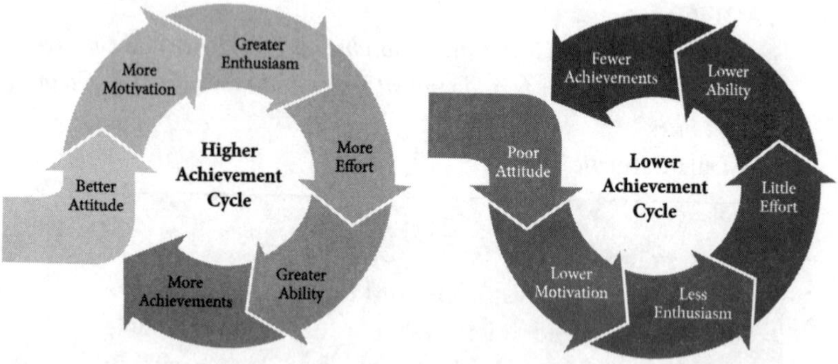

When you have a hard time feeling enthusiastic, act the part! Act enthusiastic and you'll feel enthusiastic. Feel enthusiastic and you'll BE enthusiastic. When you're excited and enthusiastic about something, you're in a position of power. You don't feel weary or hesitant, and easily move into the task.

Enthusiasm is the outward reflection of inner confidence.

Have Confidence

> *"Until you value yourself, you will not value your time. Until you value your time, you will not do anything with it."*
> — M. Scott Peck

If a job feels too big, or you are afraid you might not do a good job, remember to have confidence in yourself. Remember that confidence is not about what you know how to do, it's trusting yourself to take a new situation step-by-step, allowing yourself to make mistakes, but knowing you'll stick it out and finish the job. Every time you deliver on your own promises, your confidence will increase.

Start small

> *"Action may not always bring about happiness, but there is no happiness without action."*
> — Benjamin Disraeli

Do a small part of your task at a time. For example, *"I'll just do a mind map for now. Later, I'll start an outline."* Action is essential to overcoming procrastination – even a small step.

Check your mind

This method is adapted from an ancient Buddhist meditation technique. When you start to rationalize about why you don't need to start your task, simply say to yourself, *"action"* and then immediately move into action. Right then – pick up the pen and start making a plan, start writing, start reading. If you notice yourself losing concentration and getting involved with distractions, tell yourself *"action"* again and guide yourself back to the original task. You can gently train yourself to concentrate this way.

Change your motivation

One secret about motivation and procrastination is this: It's not that you're not motivated to do something; it's that you're motivated to do something else.

When you view motivation this way, it gives you the choice to make a change. When you find yourself procrastinating, choose to find the motivation to get important tasks done.

"You're writing the story of your life one moment at a time."
— Doc Childre

The Moral of the Story
The best time to start managing time is *before* you get behind. Studying and academics are the main priorities for your time in college, but with careful time management and by *avoiding* procrastination, you can, and should, schedule in a lot of fun.

~ Chapter Six ~
Excelling in The Classroom Without Being Grumpy, Sleepy or Dopey

You might be thinking, *"We've been studying since elementary school, so why would we need help with our study skills?"*

Most everyone has a particular set of study skills that comes naturally to them. Other skills may have been developed only with time and practice. You may have tried certain study methods and written them off because you found they didn't work for you. However, there may be other study skills that you're completely unaware of that could be of great help throughout college. Of course, some of you - and you know who you are - may never have found it necessary to develop study skills, relying instead on an ability to memorize information and learn quickly.

Campus ToolKit offers three areas of help:

1. **A Sensory Learning Styles Assessment**, to discover whether you're a *Visual, Auditory, Tactile or Kinesthetic learner*. Knowing your sensory learning style will help you choose methods of study that work for you.

   Should you have a quiet room where you can focus and study undisturbed, or should you organize study groups to learn most effectively? Would it be best for you to stand or pace while studying, perhaps with flashcards, or should you record your lectures and listen back while exercising? You'll be able to answer these questions when you take this assessment.

2. **Study Skills Assessment**
   This assessment takes a look at ten different areas that affect your potential to study, and gives you a clear understanding of areas where you are excelling, and of those where you could improve.

3. **Note Taking Help**
   Because taking notes is critical to your success in the classroom, we've included tips here on note taking. You can refer to these any time, and experiment with several styles of note taking. You can even customize your note taking for your sensory learning style.

Getting Started
The best place to start is by taking the **Sensory Learning Styles assessment**. Once you have your results, you can read all about your learning style in the following pages.

The Visual Learning Style
If you are a visual learner, you work best with information that is presented in a graphical manner. This includes written text, but also includes information on web sites, in slides or in charts. Frequently, you will remember things by "*looking*" at them in your mind. For example, you might remember reading the answer to a quiz question in a chart at the bottom of a textbook page. You'll actually be able to picture its location on that page.

Visual learners tend to prefer studying alone. For optimum studying, they also prefer quiet areas. Lots of activity and people talking around them break their concentration.

Visual Learning Study Strategies

Use flashcards to help you reduce the amount of competing information. Just put the really important things on the cards.

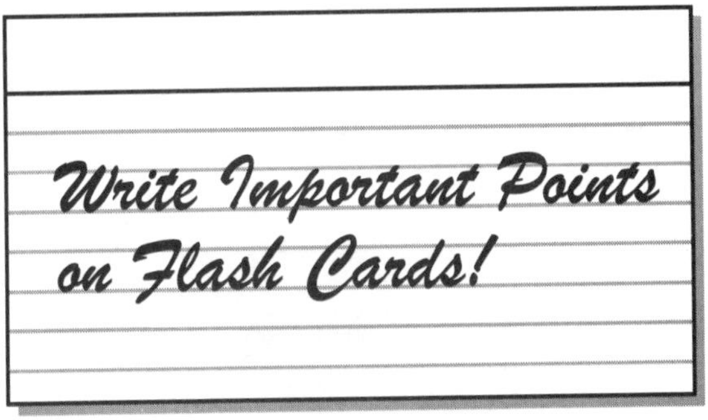

Symbols and diagrams may help you to summarize information. For example, when learning about the 5-star constellation Corvus, you might create something like this:

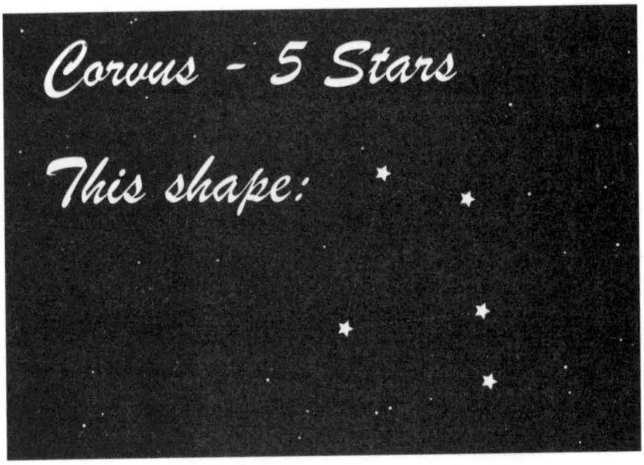

Try studying in a quiet room. Conversations around you may be particularly distracting. You may also want to study alone.

~ **QUIET PLEASE. STUDYING IN PROGRESS!**

USE HIGHLIGHTERS

This helps to pull out important information for you.

Use post-it notes to put information around your room. This works well with dates or short lists that you may need to memorize. Try posting things where you will see them multiple times per day.

When learning sequential information, create timelines or boxes and flow charts. Use white space in your notes so they don't get too cluttered.

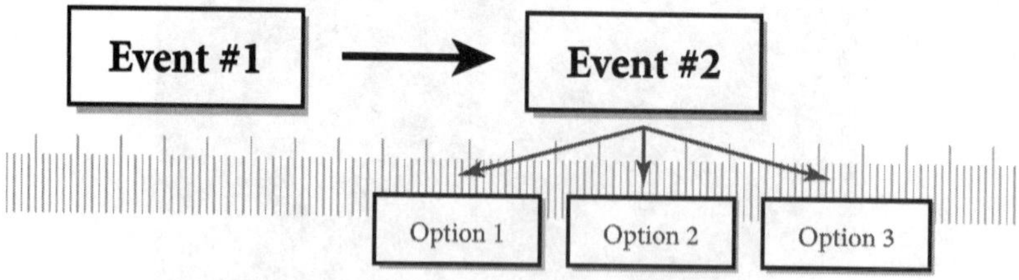

Use your imagination; create image associations in your mind.

For example:
Imagine yourself watching the attack on Pearl Harbor and see the date of the

newspaper you are holding in your hands - *December 7, 1941.*

Remember, some of these techniques will be more useful to you than others. Try them all and see what works!

The Auditory Learning Style

Auditory learners like information presented verbally. Classroom lectures and group discussions are great for them. Auditory learners also do well in study groups where they can discuss information with others. The process of hearing information and then reinforcing it by saying it out loud helps to solidify learning. Other formats that are good for auditory learners are audio recordings or even movies. When auditory learners try to remember something, many times they will be able to *"listen"* to the answers in their heads. They will hear the information as they did when they heard it from the instructor or maybe as they did when they were saying it out loud while studying.

Auditory Learning Study Strategies

- ~ Study in groups or with a partner. One of the best ways to know that you've learned the information is to be able to summarize it for someone else.

- Read important points out loud. Try recording these points so you can listen to them again.
- Make recordings of lectures. Listen to them in the car or while exercising.
- Sometimes, books on tape can be a good alternative. Just make sure you schedule plenty of time to listen to them.
- To learn sequential information, try writing the steps out first on flashcards. Then, read the cards out loud until you feel comfortable with the information. Finally, try saying the information out loud without looking at the cards. Alternatively, try explaining the information to someone else at this point.

The Tactile Learning Style

The sense of touch is vital to tactile learners. The more tactile learners can touch and feel whatever they are studying, the better they will retain the information. In lecture classes, you may find yourself taking a lot of notes and you may notice yourself pushing down hard with your pencil as you do so. The process of putting pencil to paper is actually helping you to process information. Rewriting your notes later will reinforce your learning and is a very effective study strategy for tactile learners. For the same reasons, flashcards can be very useful to you. The process of creating the flash cards will help you tease out the main themes and associated details that are important and then you can hold the cards in your hands as you study. Often, tactile learners are good with their hands and may choose to ignore instruction manuals in favor of just getting started with something new.

Tactile learners also tend to be good at interpersonal skills. Reading body language and identifying how others are feeling comes naturally to them. Consequently, relating well to your instructors will be important. If you have the opportunity to choose your classes, consider the instructor's reputation and standing among your peers as you select a course.

Tactile Learning Study Strategies

- Sit in front of the classroom and take lots of notes. The act of note taking will help you to retain information.

- Rewrite the notes you have taken in class. This will help you clarify the main points and the process of rewriting will solidify the learning for you.
- Rewrite or copy important information from your textbook to your notes.
- Write key words, make pictures, etc. in the margins of your textbook.
- When studying, you don't need to sit still. Especially with notes and flashcards you can walk, pace, etc.
- Instead of laying your textbook on a table or bed to read, try to hold it in your hands.
- When reading, move your fingers across the page. This is helpful as you try to process difficult passages.
- If possible, find alternative ways to get the information from the world around you. Build models, use flashcards, etc.
- To learn sequential information, create flashcards for each step and place them in order on a table. Keep placing the cards in order on the table until you've mastered the information.
- Get a stress ball or something you can discretely work with in your free hand while you're in class taking notes. Sometimes giving your hands something to do can help your mind focus on the instructor.

The Kinesthetic Learning Style

Kinesthetic learners are often challenged by traditional classroom settings because classrooms are seldom *"active"* environments. Kinesthetic learners gather information in a hands-on manner, whether that is during lab classes, in-class activities and demonstrations, or on field trips. In lecture classes, you may find yourself fidgeting or tapping your fingers. Movement is key to your mental processing so you need to find strategies to incorporate that into the traditional classroom environment. Often, kinesthetic learners are good with their hands and may choose to ignore instruction manuals in favor of just getting started with something new.

Kinesthetic Learning Study Strategies

- If you have the opportunity to choose your professors, ask around to find out who teaches in an engaging style that will work for you. Other kinesthetic learners will be sure to remember instructors they've had who create active classrooms.

- Sit in front of the classroom and take lots of notes. The act of note taking will help you to retain information.
- Write key words, make pictures, etc.
- Participate in any field trips that are offered.
- Spend extra time in the lab portion of class.
- When studying, you don't need to sit still. Especially with notes and flashcards you can walk, pace, etc. while you say the material out loud.
- If possible, find alternative ways to get the information from the world around you. Build models, go to museums, use flashcards, etc.
- To learn sequential information, create flashcards for each step and place them in order on a table. Keep placing the cards in order on the table until you've mastered the information.
- Rewrite or copy important information from your textbook to your notes. This is an active process and will help you retain information. Copying information is another reason to use flashcards.
- Make recordings of important information and then listen to them while exercising or driving.
- Get a stress ball or something you can discretely work with in your hands while you're in class. Sometimes giving your hands something to do can help your mind focus on the instructor.
- If you have trouble maintaining focus while you study, try scheduling multiple, shorter study sessions interspersed with some form of physical activity instead of attempting one long study session.
- When studying, try to imagine putting theory into practice. Create case studies to help you learn abstract concepts. You can even do this when trying to remember concrete facts. For example, when trying to learn the date of the attack on Pearl Harbor you could think about the fact that it was a Sunday. Ask yourself why the Japanese might have picked a Sunday morning for the attack. You could contrast the weather in Hawaii in December to the weather we

typically associate with Christmas. When you have to answer the question on the test, chances are that you'll remember these scenarios and that will trigger the date for you. There are many different scenarios you can create as you try to commit something to memory.

Words and Phrases Used by Each Learning Style

Visual	Auditory	Tactile/Kinesthetic
Appears to me	All ears	All washed up
Bird's-eye view	Call on	Boils down to
Bright	Clear as a bell	Catch on
Catch a glimpse of	Crying out to me	Come to grips with
Clear	Deaf	Concrete
Clear-cut	Describe in detail	Feel
Dawn	Hear what I'm saying?	Firm foundation
Dim view	Earful	Floating on air
Eye to eye	Give me your ear	Get a handle on
Focused	Harmonize	Get hold of
Foggy	Hear	Get in touch with
Get an eyeful	Hush	Get the drift of
Having a bright future	Idle talk	Grapple with a problem
Hazy	It sounds good to me	Grasp a concept
I see what you mean	Listen	Grope for an answer
I'll look into it	Loud and clear	Hand in hand
Illuminate	Make music	Hang in there
Imagine	Melody	Hard
In light of	On another note	Heated argument
In person	Outspoken	Hold it
In view of	Purrs like a kitten	Lay the cards on the table
Looks like	Quiet as a mouse	Make contact
Mental image	Resonate	Make a connection
Mind's eye	Rings a bell	Pull some strings
Naked eye	Roar	Scrape
Paint a picture	Silence	Sharp as a tack
Pretty as a picture	Something tells me	Slipped my mind
Reveal	Sound	Smooth operator
Scope out	Squeak	Solid
See to it	Tell	Start from scratch
Short-sighted	To tell the truth	Stiff upper lip
Showing off	Tune in/out	Tap into
Sight for sore eyes	Unheard of	Throw out
Take a peek	Voiced an opinion	Touch
Tunnel vision	Within earshot	Underhanded
View		Unfeeling

Study Skills Assessment

To evaluate your studies skills, we've provided an online **Study Skills assessment**. The purpose of this assessment is to highlight potential problem areas. When you've finished, you'll know exactly what areas you can improve upon for better results in the classroom.

Flash Point!

Go online now to take the assessment. When you have your results, you'll see that we've provided links to information in our online Knowledge Modules that address each and every aspect of the assessment. The modules also give you ideas to improve your study skills and get the most out of school.

The assessment results and the online information are separated into ten different study skill areas that have been found to influence your academic success:

1. **Anxiety** – For times when you feel overwhelmed with worry and nervousness.
2. **Attitude** – Relating your college experience to getting what you want in life.
3. **Concentration** – Finding ways to eliminate distractions and learning to focus your mind at will.
4. **Information Processing** – To help reduce the amount of memorizing needed to study effectively.
5. **Motivation and Goal Setting** – Finding your priorities and values in life and discovering goals you want to work toward.
6. **Self-Testing** – How to know when you fully understand material, and determine when you're *ready* to take a test.
7. **Selecting Main Ideas** – Learning to identify main points without getting bogged down in supporting details.
8. **Study Aids** – A comprehensive list of study aids with suggestions of how to find the best ones for your learning style and personality type.
9. **Time Management** – Overcoming procrastination and gaining control over time.
10. **Testing Strategies** – Preparing for a test, finding the right frame of mind for exams, and reasoning through questions.

Although we've been learning all our lives, many of us were never actually taught how to study and process information. Throughout our online **Study Skills Knowledge Modules** we've included exercises and asked thought-provoking questions to help you discover ways of studying and learning that work *for you*. You may be surprised to find that you've already got better skills than you thought you did.

Take Note!

Note taking forms the core of your study techniques and getting it right can make studying a lot easier in college. There are many techniques to take notes, and finding one that works for you is as easy as experimenting with a few methods and seeing the result. We've included three specific note taking systems for you to try, including the Cornell Method, using an outline form, or mind mapping. It might be worth trying all three until you find the one that works best for you.

All three methods for note taking work best with a loose-leaf notebook, so that you can add, delete or rearrange pages. At the top of each page, it's helpful to note the date, course, and names of any guest speakers that presented that day – including other students.

5 R and Cornell Method

This is a popular and very effective form of note taking, developed by Walter Pauk, a Cornell Professor. It saves time by not requiring lengthy re-writes of notes. All the work is done in the initial lecture or reading session and during a short review.

For our purposes, we are blending the Cornell method with the 5 R method:

Record, Reduce, Recite, Reflect, Review.

Some bookstores sell a Cornell notebook that is already ruled for this use. Otherwise, you can easily do it yourself.

1. Separate your page by drawing a vertical line approximately 2 $1/2$ inches from the left-hand side. This will leave a six inch section on the right.
2. At the bottom, section off one inch for a page summary.

Step 1: *Record*
When taking notes in class, write in the bigger section on the right-hand side. Leave plenty of space between each point your instructor makes, because you'll be filling in later.

As soon as possible after class, or at the very latest before your next lecture, fill in any incomplete sentences and rephrase disjointed thoughts in the space you left between each point on the right-hand side.

Step 2: *Reduce*
For every significant bit of information, write a *cue* in the left-hand column. This is where you will devise questions that the notes answer (think *"Jeopardy"*). You can also write key words and phrases.

The one-inch section at the bottom is used for a summary. Think of one or two sentences that review the material on the page. The summary section serves two important functions:

1. Acts as a quick reference when looking for specific information later.
2. Forces you to view the material in a relational sense – the bigger picture. The summary should help you see how specific facts fit into broader theories.

Anytime you want to review your notes, cover the right side with a thick piece of paper, and use the notes in the left-hand column to think through concepts.

Step 3: *Recite*
With the right-hand side covered with a blank piece of paper, use your cues to talk through, and reiterate main points out loud. Say the cue on the left out loud, and then say as much of the information on the right-hand side as you can recall.

When you have said as much as you can remember, remove the blank piece of paper and see if you covered all of the points. Saying things out loud enhances your learning process and helps commit information to long-term memory.

Does the idea of speaking out loud make you uncomfortable? Bear in mind that it is the most effective study method available, whether you are alone, teaching a friend, or rephrasing material into your own words with a study partner. It's also the fastest way to learn, leaving you more time for other things!

Step 4: *Reflect*
Think it over.

- ~ How do your notes relate to what you knew before?
- ~ What connections can you make to previous material?
- ~ How can you make this new information meaningful?
- ~ What material could you use for essays? Make a note and create a list of topics you can develop.

Step 5: *Review*
Review your notes at your next study session, before your next lecture, before reading new material, and when studying for tests.

Taking notes on your laptop
The Cornell method works very effectively on a laptop by using tables in your word processing programs.

Here's a smaller sample of how it would look:

Course:		Date:		Guest Speaker's Name:	
Put in key words, phrases and questions that your notes on the right answer.		*Put your notes in this area. Leave lots of space between your notes.*			
Summary:	*Think of one or two sentences to review the material on this page. This is the big picture area.*				

Or, use our template online. You can find it under the Tools > Exercises menu.

When you've finished taking notes, create cues and summarize. Then print and proceed to the recite, reflect, and review steps.

Outline Method

This method works when you're very good at note taking and organizing material. If your lecture is presented in an outline format, it will be easier to do. It can be difficult when an instructor bounces around between topics or the lecture goes too quickly.

Listen and then write points in an organized manner. Don't worry about using roman numerals, numbers or letters. Just use dashes or indentations to show that material belongs to a group of facts or an idea.

The more specific the fact, the farther you indent to show relationships.

For example:

Ego

- Reliant upon:
  - Having a skill (math, sports, art, etc.)
  - Knowing how to do something well
  - A particular possession
  - Having an innate trait such as beauty, wealth of family, or intelligence
  - Becomes threatened when:
    - Skill is not called for or necessary
    - Possession is irrelevant or unknown
    - Innate quality is not important in a situation
- Egotistical person relates to others by:
  - Comparing skills
  - Belittling or pointing out their own excellence over others'
  - Bragging, finding ways to exhibit skills or traits (showing off)

Mapping technique

If the structure of the previous two methods gets you down, try mapping. This method looks similar to a mind map. Later, you can highlight or color code related idea clusters.

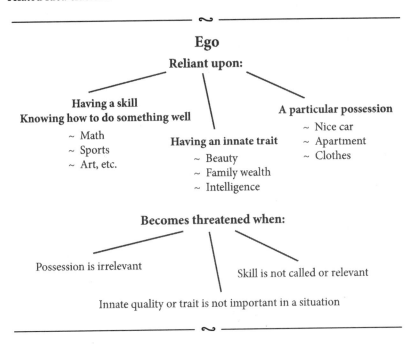

Ego

Reliant upon:

Having a skill
Knowing how to do something well

~ Math
~ Sports
~ Art, etc.

Having an innate trait

~ Beauty
~ Family wealth
~ Intelligence

A particular possession

~ Nice car
~ Apartment
~ Clothes

Becomes threatened when:

Possession is irrelevant

Skill is not called or relevant

Innate quality or trait is not important in a situation

Take control of your study time and customize your note taking. By making just a small time investment and experimenting with some of the suggestions we've made to find study methods based on your learning type, you'll save more time than you could ever imagine.

The Moral of the Story

Determining the study skills that come naturally to you means you'll save time and learn more quickly and efficiently. Knowing whether you learn best by listening, seeing, touching or doing will help you choose the most effective ways to study.

~ Chapter Seven ~
Mirror, Mirror: The DISC Assessment

Do you ever wonder why:

- ~ You seem to *"click"* right away with some people, and others you just don't get?
- ~ No matter how hard you try with some, they seem to misunderstand you and get annoyed?
- ~ Some people are easily stressed and can't keep up with the pace of change, while others seem to thrive on the challenge of change and deadlines?

- Some people have no patience for detail and only see the big picture? While others get so bogged down in the detail that they can't see the big picture at all?

What about how some people get bored easily and never seem to stick with anything for long, while others do the same things their whole lives, never wanting to try something new?

How can you get along so well with some instructors, feeling like everything you say is what they want to hear - and get the feeling that with other instructors, you only get on their nerves?

Many of these differences are explained by our behavioral styles. If you have taken the DISC assessment and you know your DISC type, you have one of the most effective tools available to help you understand how you communicate. If you haven't taken the assessment yet, you're only 24 questions away from knowing, which of four types you are:

D Driver	I Influencer	S Stabilizer	C Conscientious

But how does your type interact with others? In this chapter, we'll talk about:

- How DISC works and the different temperaments of the various types.
- Why you might easily relate to some people and have a hard time with others.
- How to speed-read the DISC type of others.
- Which types might naturally get along.
- Which types enhance each other's distinct skills and why.
- How knowing someone's DISC type can help you better identify with:
    - Roommates
    - Parents
    - Friends
    - Instructors

And finally, how you benefit a team: what you have to offer that others may not.

First, we'll give you a quick understanding of the DISC, and how it works.

Learning the basics of DISC

DISC is based on four basic behaviors that can be found universally in people. Everyone has all four tendencies, but in varying degrees of intensity. If you look on the example DISC results chart below, you'll see the degree to which this person has each quality.

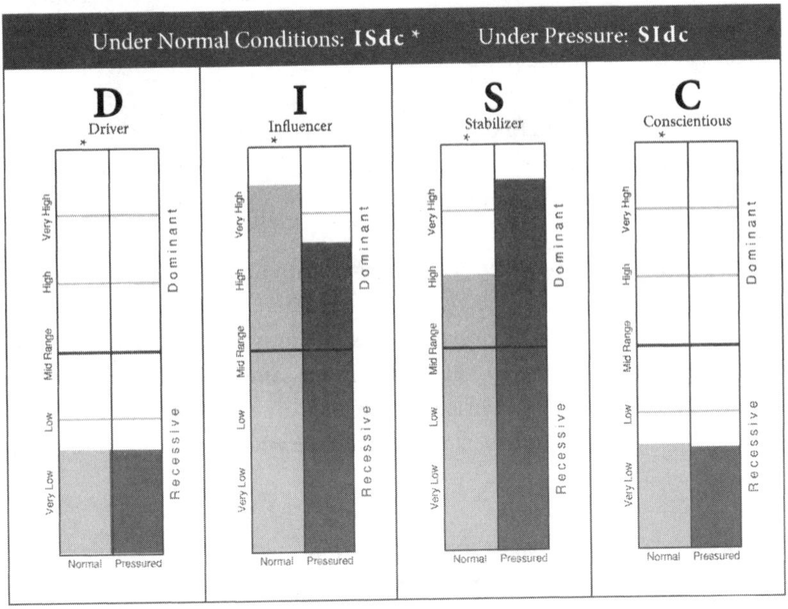

The traits above the mid line of the chart are considered your most active, and contribute the most to your general behavior.

Now, notice the top area of the chart. You'll see two combinations of the four letters; one for normal conditions, and one for when you're under pressure.

- ~ Any behavior above mid range on the chart is depicted in your type with a capital letter; any behavior below the mid range is indicated with a small letter.

For example:

Under Normal Conditions: *ISdc*
I and *S* are dominant traits, *d* and *c* are recessive.

~ Behaviors under normal conditions are shown on the chart on the previous page in a light grey color. Your behavior when you're under pressure is shown in a dark grey color. Many people only experience a slight shift in their behavior when under pressure and others can experience more of a change.

In our example, the Under Normal Conditions result of *ISdc* become an *Under Pressure SIdc*. The trait that changed most for this person was a marked increase in the *S* temperament.

~ Some people will find that they only have one dominant behavior above the mid line. Most people have a combination of two and a few have three. Nobody has all four as dominant traits.

What's the difference between *"normal circumstances and "under pressure"*?
Most people experience a change in behavior when they're stressed or under pressure in some way. Usually, certain traits become stronger and others lessen. For example, as we just noted, the person in the sample on the previous page shows signs of more *S* characteristics when they are under pressure. We'll talk specifically about what to expect from each type when under pressure a little later in this chapter.

Next we'll take a brief look at the four types. Remember, most people are not just one type, but a combination of two. However, it is usually easiest to guess a person's single most dominant trait. For example, we might refer to a chatty person as being a High-I. Or we might call someone with a strong attention to detail a High-C person.

Driver

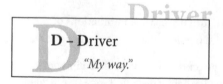

D - Driver
"My way."

These types typically like to be in charge. They're dominant, direct, decisive, and demanding. They are often described as innovative, self-reliant, energetic and optimistic. They function well under heavy workloads, accept risks, and overcome obstacles. They are willing to speak out, and readily accept challenges without fear. They are also described as impatient, competitive, forceful, and sometimes blunt or egotistical.

Drivers are **task-oriented**.

Motivated by:

~ New challenges
~ Control
~ Freedom from the mundane or routine
~ Change
~ Authority
~ Choices, rather than ultimatums

Basic approach:

~ Direct, forthright, to-the-point, formal

Under Pressure:

~ Works hard and maintains focus
~ Can become domineering and impatient

Measures progress by:

~ Results

Fears:

~ Being taken advantage of
~ Feeling stupid or slow on the uptake
~ Loss of control

I – Influencer

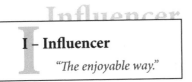

"The enjoyable way."

These types like communicating with others. They love an audience, and often seek recognition and approval. They're socially very active, enthusiastic and optimistic. They're often described as inspiring, persuasive, talkative and impulsive. They rarely like to be alone, are easily excited and confident. They make creative problem solvers, often work as peacemakers, and readily encourage others. They can be very competitive and overbearing at times. They can also be described as impatient, inconsistent, and manipulative.

Influencing types are **people-oriented**.

Motivated by:

~ Acceptance
~ Approval
~ Opportunities to motivate others
~ Praise
~ Recognition
~ A chance to communicate their ideas

Basic approach:

~ Informal, indirect, communicative, friendly

Under Pressure:

~ Talks it out, lets off steam
~ Can become emotional and disorganized

Measures progress by:

~ Praise, all parties being happy

Fears:

~ Rejection
~ Looking bad or wrong

Stabilizer

S – Stabilizer

"The safe way."

These types are loyal, dependable and friendly. They're also cooperative, practicing patience and persistence in almost any situation. They like harmony, and become distressed about confrontation in any form. They work best under stable conditions and are comfortable with routine, processes and procedures. If something needs to change, they appreciate an easy transition. They're often described as good listeners, tolerant, and empathetic. Steady, predictable, security-oriented and concentrative are also used to describe stabilizers. They can be *"too"* hospitable, slow to change, possessive and submissive as well. They are known for holding grudges – an *S* will never forget an argument, although they may not say so.

Stabilizing types are **people-oriented.**

Motivated by:

~ Security and safety
~ Appreciation
~ Recognition for hard work
~ Close relationships
~ Stability
~ Consistent, familiar patterns

Basic approach:

~ Friendly, amiable, indirect, open and personal

Under Pressure:

~ Avoids conflict, solicits opinions from others, remains open and patient
~ Can tend to conform for the sake of peace, or become indecisive

Measures progress by:

~ Appreciation received

Fears:

~ Sudden change without warning
~ Fights or confrontation
~ Personal rejection

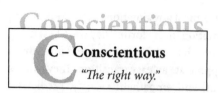

C – Conscientious

"The right way."

These types value competence, quality and accuracy. They are generally private individuals. They're often described as compliant, cautious and calculating. They usually have high standards, are diplomatic, and detail-oriented. They believe in organization, planning their work, and doing things right. They are sometimes described as overly precise, critical, picky, and rigid.

Conscientious types are **task-oriented.**

Motivated by:

~ High Standards
~ Detail
~ Dependability
~ Accuracy
~ Correctness
~ Limited social interaction

Basic approach:

~ Direct, functional, correct and structured

Under Pressure:

~ Dislike being forced to cut corners or save time under pressure
~ Can be stubborn or withdrawn

Measures progress by:

~ Getting it right

Fears:

~ Making mistakes
~ Criticism of their work or ideas
~ Lack of standards

By reading over these descriptions of the four types, you might recognize why you scored the way you did. Remember that most people are a combination of all behaviors to varying degrees.

You may also see characteristics of friends and family in these types.

There's you, and then there's you under pressure

Looking at your DISC results, you'll see that when you're under pressure your results shift slightly. Depending on your unique result, you might change a little more or a little less than others under stress. It's helpful to be aware of how you might change and how those around you might act under pressure. By learning how your personality type reacts under pressure, you'll be better able to spot the warning signs of when you're just not yourself, and take more care in your behavior.

D – Drivers under pressure

As a driver, you may have a natural tendency to believe you can control your surroundings. You may also be results-driven and may not like getting bogged down in details. Drivers are also impatient, so you might find that your patience is even less when you're under pressure. Drivers are also very competitive and that part of you can be amplified when you're stressed out.

If you start to feel negative about being in college or about certain classes, relax, try not to be quite so goal-focused. Find a way to maintain perspective. When you're in a good space, you can be very motivating to others, and this motivation can help people immensely.

I – Influencers under pressure

As an influencer, you enjoy being with others, and are often very active socially. If you're feeling frustrated or negative for any reason, try talking it out - just be sure the people you talk to are constructive, and really want the best for you. If you're down and you feel better after talking to someone, that's a good person to talk to. If you feel uneasy, or even worse after talking to someone, avoid confiding in him or her again. For example, if you're trying to improve your beliefs about your own control of your destiny, and you feel these beliefs may have come from your family, try talking to an instructor or school counselor who has seen, first hand, success stories for someone in a situation like yours.

Like drivers, you can also be very motivating to others, making you a big help to your friends and classmates. For classes that you don't like or aren't interested in, try organizing study groups. It will make your study time easier, and more fun. Influencers often have an inherent dislike of details, so try using your interaction with others to help you get through the boring stuff.

S – Stabilizers under pressure

Stabilizers under pressure can become very independent. They are also very comfortable with routine, which can cause them to be resistant to change when under pressure. Because of this, you can feel highly uncomfortable when a lot of change is happening - and this first year of college brings the biggest changes of all! When you recognize these behaviors, you can be aware of how you treat others around you, so that you don't take out your frustrations on them. You may find yourself frustrated with everything new in your life, but keep a positive outlook and draw on your strength to change.

Remember when you feel this way that you're the one who is in control and there is no race to achieve your goals. Goals, values, and priorities are process-oriented, so take things at your own pace.

C – Conscientious under pressure

Conscientious personality types like privacy, and like to control their surroundings. As a *C* you are probably excellent at collecting information, and benefit from having time to think.

The opposite can be true when you're under pressure; when you aren't given enough time to think, you can feel pressured, and you will react negatively. When this happens, you may become moody, or even experience emotional lows or depression. It's important to acknowledge the source of these problems, and find a solution. Just knowing why you're feeling this way will probably be of some comfort.

How your DISC type can affect your success in school

D – Drivers

Because you are generally after a result, you might find yourself scoffing at the micro-goals and detail involved with creating new goals. Drivers can be impatient, and you'll probably want to dive right in and not take the time to plan. Try to resist this temptation – you'll get where you're going faster by planning. Your innate competitiveness can also be amplified when you're working toward a goal.

You can equally find that you lose concentration when you have to wait too long for *"the point."* (If you can relate to this in lectures, use the active listening technique that can be found in our Study Aids Knowledge Module online to help you focus.) When studying, starting from *"the main point"* and working backwards toward the supporting details might be less frustrating for you.

Finally, you might find that because you focus on the big picture and aren't as interested in the detailed steps needed to achieve the big picture, you might have a tendency not to finish projects or study thoroughly. It might be valuable for you to create specific, bulleted lists to study. Or, as we suggested above, try working backwards. Create flow charts and diagrams that start with the end result or main information pieces and back it up with as many facts as you can.

I – Influencers

As an influencer, you enjoy being with others, and are often very active socially. Try organizing study groups, since you will thrive in this atmosphere – but be sure you gain information and don't just socialize! Practice listening at these gatherings, and maybe talking less. If you are competitive, remember that study groups are not a competition of who knows more - your benefit will come from hearing other approaches and increasing your knowledge. There is a saying that goes: "*A good listener is not only popular everywhere, but after awhile he knows something!*" Influencers often have an inherent dislike of details, so try using your interaction with others to help you get through the boring stuff.

Another issue *"High-I"* people face is the natural tendency to digress from a main topic easily, with your concentration following whatever is happening around you. Be sure you don't lose the main topic altogether.

S – Stabilizers

As a stabilizer you tend to be very independent, and are very comfortable with routine. This personality type is well suited to studying from a textbook. By developing a reliable system for taking notes, you'll be able to confidently depend on your own notes as study aids.

Stabilizers are prone to becoming drowsy when sitting, so be sure to break up your study sessions with physical activity. You can also make activity-based study aids, like creating your own flash cards that you can use while you walk or pace.

Although you work well on your own, try attending study groups and review sessions to gather another perspective and gain information. You'll benefit just by listening, but don't be afraid to ask questions or contribute – your organized thinking could be a big help to fellow students!

C – Conscientious

Conscientious personality types tend to value privacy and like to control their surroundings. As a *C* you are probably excellent at collecting information, and benefit from having time to think.

Conscientious types will probably be most comfortable finding a quiet, private space in which to study. C's operate very well from a plan, so schedule time to develop an outline or game plan before actually studying. But be careful! C's have a tendency to spend too much time on detail. A rough outline will do! These types can get bogged down in triple-checking material, concentrating on the details instead of getting the job done. You may benefit from learning to identify main points better. The Selecting Main Ideas section of the Study Skills Knowledge Module online can help you do that.

Setting goals can be another area where you have the potential to spin out – concentrating so much on the detail that you never take action. When setting goals, be sure you actually start down your list of micro-goals and realize that you will learn best by doing. Remember the *Ready, Fire, Aim* theory.

Give study sessions and review sessions a try, because they are a valuable way to check that you're on the right track with your studies.

Meeting new people

"I really relate to this person!"

Put simply, types whose dominant behaviors are close to each other in DISC get along better. For example, D&I make a good team, as well as I&S types. This can explain why you sometimes meet someone and *"click"* right away.

"I don't get this person at all!"
Of course, there are times when you just can't seem to relate or find any middle ground with someone. Awkward silences, misunderstandings, and halting conversations make the experience uncomfortable. Often you might feel you are just operating at two different speeds.

Chances are these people are not near you in DISC. You may be a *D* and they're an *S*, or you're an *I* and they're a *C*. D's and C's also don't tend to *"get"* each other, having very different values.

By the way, this is true for you also! If you have two dominant traits that are not near each other, for example, both a *D* and an *S* above the line, then there is a good chance that you'll behave inconsistently at times. It's just these opposing behavior characteristics each trying to get their way.

Flash Point!
When opposites attract
This doesn't mean you can't get along with dissimilar types – many people are able to overcome - and even embrace - their differences. They learn from each other and develop lasting, rewarding relationships.

Everyone has strengths and weaknesses, and working together can help you complement each other's distinct skills. They may also bring an understanding and perspective to situations that you may lack.

Relating to other people
Here's a quick guide to see how different types work together and relate. Try doing this comparison with your roommate and friends to see the behavior

dynamic of your relationship.

To compare two people that have both taken the DISC assessment, print out the assessment results and identify the most dominant behavior. This will be the highest column on the DISC chart. If you are just looking at their letter scores without the chart, the most dominant trait is the first letter on the left.

We've also got an easy online tool to do this for you, and will give you even more detail about how you and someone else work together. It's called the DISC Compatibility Analyzer. If you'd like to see a side-by-side comparison of your type and a friend or roommate's, you can enter your name, and search for friends who have also taken the test to find out how you'll work together. This can be found online under the tools menu.

To check compatibility with someone whose chart you haven't seen, read on to learn how to determine someone's type, or use our online DISC Speed Reader under the tools menu.

If you are a D:

D & D

What works:

- ~ Working together toward common goals.
- ~ Working together with well-defined roles, and specific areas of authority.

When working together:

- ~ These two types both want to be in charge.
- ~ This can result in arguments and tension.

Challenges & opportunities for growth:

- ~ Two D's can learn to put their egos and control issues aside for the purposes of a greater goal.
- ~ Opportunity to see their own tendencies and learn to manage their attitudes.

D & I

What works:

- Influencing types provide great encouragement to drivers.
- Drivers provide direction and follow-through to influencers.

When working or studying together:

- The *I* can sometimes feel the *D* is too demanding and may resent being told what to do.
- *D* types can sometimes feel the *I* talks too much and doesn't focus.

Challenges & opportunities for growth:

- Both of these types are assertive and demanding, and may need to clearly define their roles.
- I's can learn: less charm; more work. D's can learn to lighten up and have fun.

D & S

What works:

- Usually a very easy pairing for work - may be more difficult personally.
- S's provide stability; the D's provide motivation.

When working together:

- D's generally like to be in charge and S's are usually happy to take a back seat.
- S's can generate detailed plans to follow on from D's thrust and drive

Challenges & opportunities for growth:

- Can find it hard to respect each other.
- D's can learn to slow down and *"smell the roses."*
- S's can be motivated and can learn assertiveness.

D & C

What works:

~ These two work very well together on teams and toward goals.

When working together:

~ D's determined drive is enhanced by C's structure and attention to detail.

Challenges & opportunities for growth:

~ C's can learn to break out of routine and take a few risks.

~ D's can learn to consider facts and think before they leap.

~ Since both of these types are task-oriented, they can benefit from having a people-oriented *I* or *S* as part of their team.

If you are an I:

I & D

What works:

~ Influencing types provide great encouragement to drivers

~ Drivers provide direction and follow-through to influencers

When working or studying together:

~ The *I* can sometimes feel the *D* is too demanding and may resent being told what to do

~ *D* types can sometimes feel the *I* talks too much and doesn't focus

Challenges & opportunities for growth:

~ Both of these types are assertive and demanding and may need to clearly define their roles.

~ I's can learn: Less charm; more work. D's can learn to lighten up and have fun.

I & I

What works:

~ Both influencers will enjoy each other personally.

~ Will motivate each other and find each other stimulating and fun.

When working together:

~ These two types may tend to talk and dream more than work.

~ They may have a tendency to let deadlines slide, or make big promises to each other and never follow through.

Challenges & opportunities for growth:

~ Set goals, stick to them, and get results from your many ideas

I & S

What works:

~ Stabilizers provide excellent support to the idea-generating influencer.

~ Stabilizers also tend to ground the influencer, providing more meaningful communication.

When working together:

~ Stabilizers help keep the influencer focused on their goals.

~ Influencers provide infinite ideas.

Challenges & opportunities for growth:

~ In relationships, influencers may want more social interaction than stabilizers.

~ Stabilizers can learn assertiveness from influencers.

~ Influencers can learn to appreciate a solid, meaningful relationship.

I & C

What works:

- ~ These types can combine their outlook and skills for a good team when differences are put aside.
- ~ Each has very different skills to bring to a project.

When working together:

- ~ By splitting duties, I's can focus on people, C's can focus on facts.
- ~ I's can stimulate C's and C's can ground the *I*.

Challenges & opportunities for growth:

- ~ *I* types can learn to gather more facts and be more precise.
- ~ Conscientious types can learn to let go of perfectionism and can be motivated by the *I*.
- ~ Influencing types can learn to slow down and think things through.

If you are an S:

S & D

What works:

- ~ Usually a very easy pairing for work - may be more difficult personally.
- ~ S's provides stability; the D's provide motivation.

When working together:

- ~ D's generally like to be in charge and S's are usually happy to take a back seat.
- ~ S's can generate detailed plans to follow on from D's thrust and drive.

Challenges & opportunities for growth:

- ~ Can find it hard to respect each other.
- ~ D's can learn to slow down and *"smell the roses"*.
- ~ S's can be motivated and can learn assertiveness.

S & I

What works:

- Stabilizers provide excellent support to the idea-generating influencer.
- Stabilizers also tend to ground the influencer, providing more meaningful communication.

When working together:

- Stabilizers help keep the influencer focused on their goals.
- Influencers provide infinite ideas.

Challenges & opportunities for growth:

- In relationships, influencers may want more social interaction than stabilizers.
- Stabilizers can learn assertiveness from influencers.
- Influencers can learn to appreciate a solid, meaningful relationship.

S & S

What works:

- Two S's can form lifelong friendships and can bond very deeply.

When working together:

- Both S's can be resistant to change and can impede progress together.
- Ideas can take too long to come to fruition.

Challenges & opportunities for growth:

- Together these types can gently learn to overcome their challenges.

S & C

What works:

- Can create a great working relationship because they both have excellent follow-through skills and usually don't shy away from hard work.

When working together:

~ Both styles are passive, but can create a good team for follow-through.

~ S's and C's can usually agree upon, create, and follow through on a detailed plan without conflict.

~ C's can assure quality and provide objectivity.

Challenges & opportunities for growth:

~ In a relationship, these types may misunderstand each other on an emotional level

~ Clearly communicating feelings and intents can avoid this, but it may be difficult for both of these types to address

If you are a C:

C & D

What works:

~ These two work very well together on teams and toward goals.

When working together:

~ D's determined drive is enhanced by C's structure and attention to detail.

Challenges & opportunities for growth:

~ C's can learn to break out of routine and take a few risks.

~ D's can learn to consider facts, and think before they leap.

~ Since both of these types are task-oriented, they can benefit from having a people-oriented *I* or *S* as part of their team.

C & I

What works:

~ These types can combine their outlook and skills for a good team when differences are put aside.

~ Each has a very different type of skill to bring to a project.

When working together:

~ By splitting duties, I's can focus on people, C's can focus on facts.

~ I's can stimulate C's and C's can ground the *I*.

Challenges & opportunities for growth:

~ *I* types can learn to gather more facts and be more precise.

~ Conscientious types can learn to let go of perfectionism and can be motivated by the *I*.

~ Influencing types can learn to slow down and think things through.

C & S

What works:

~ Can create a great working relationship because they both have excellent follow-through skills and usually don't shy away from hard work.

When working together:

~ Both styles are passive, but can create a good team for follow-through.

~ S's and C's usually create and agree on a detailed plan, C's can assure quality and provide objectivity.

Challenges & opportunities for growth:

~ In a relationship, these types may misunderstand each other on an emotional level.

~ Clearly communicating feelings and intents can avoid this, but it may be difficult for both of these types to address.

C & C

What works:

~ This meeting of minds can provide ideas and work of incredible quality.

When working together:

~ May have a tendency to be competitive, each wanting to have the best idea or the most knowledge.

Challenges & opportunities for growth:

~ See your own tendencies and refocus on the job at hand – not one-upping each other.
~ Be mindful of deadlines.
~ Your competitive pursuit of perfection may cause you to lose sight of time.

Identifying behavior styles of others

Speed-Reading DISC types

It can often – but not always – be very simple to identify a person's primary DISC type. Use our online DISC Speed Reader, or work through the process using one of the two options here:

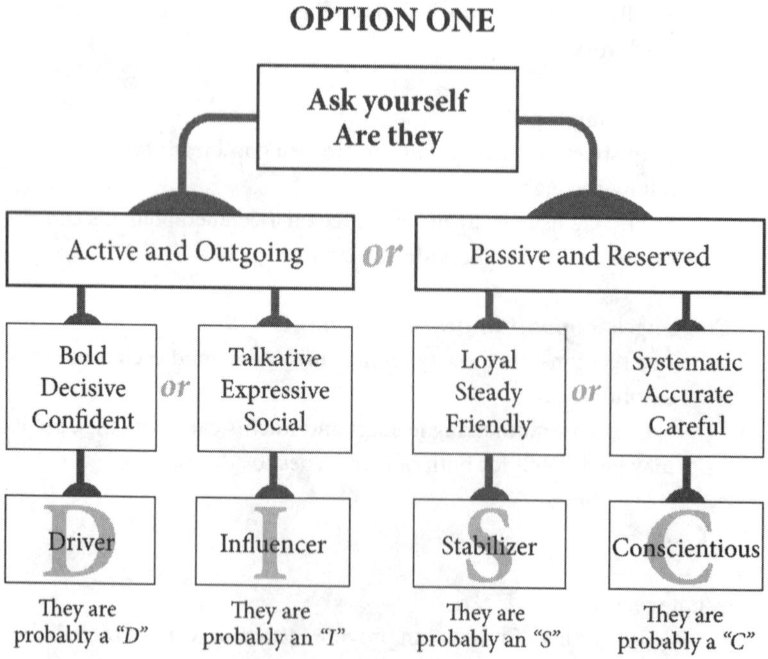

OPTION TWO

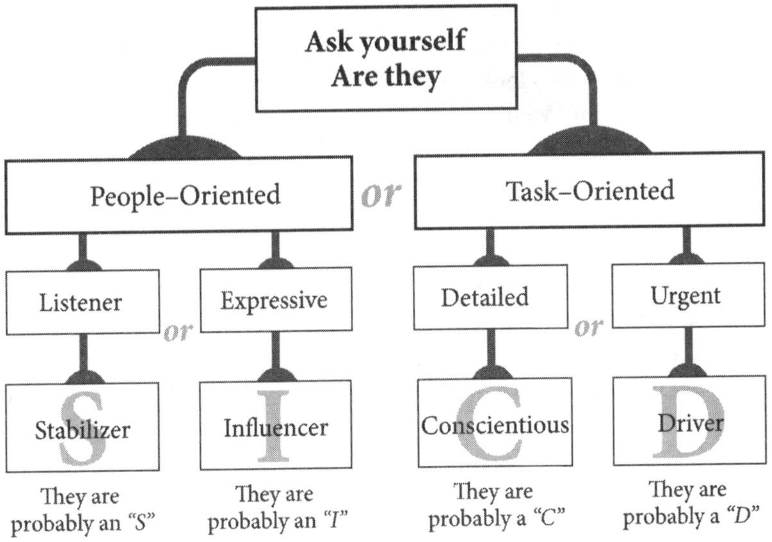

After you've determined someone's most dominant behavior, you can sometimes determine the secondary behavior by asking yourself which one of the following is the person's next most dominant quality? Remember that you can't double up on the letters. For example, if the most dominant behavior is *D*, you can't use *D* again.

Are they direct, bold and decisive?
They're probably a "*D*"

Are they verbal, social, and spontaneous?
They're probably an "*I*"

Are they loyal, perceptive, and process-focused?
They're probably an "*S*"

Finally, if they're detailed, serious, and quality-driven,
They're probably a "*C*"

Other signs to look for when identifying DISC types:

Body language / Appearance:

It is sometimes possible to find clues to help identify types from the way people look. However, it's usually more accurate to base your conclusions on their actual behaviors – looks can be deceiving… and everyone can have an "*off*" day. Think about your friends, family, or your roommate and see if you can spot the signs.

Drivers

Look for these signs:

~ May look very busy
~ Walks quickly
~ Comes on strong
~ Often appears to be in a hurry
~ Often takes charge
~ Can be fidgety and impatient

Influencers

Look for these signs:

~ Smiles often
~ Friendly looking, outgoing
~ Dressed well – may want to stand out
~ Frequent use of facial expressions and hand-movements
~ Enthusiastic
~ Impulsive
~ Shows emotion

Stabilizers

Look for these signs:

~ May look shy or unsure of themselves
~ Dresses conservatively - may want to blend-in
~ Very warm and friendly when speaking to you
~ May not be comfortable speaking in front of a group
~ Patient
~ Easy-going

Conscientious

Look for these signs:

~ Often looks serious
~ May not be overly interested in what's going on around them
~ May seem hard to get to know
~ Usually remains uninterested in elaborate presentations
~ Doesn't seem to care about bells and whistles, or anything superficial
~ Uses few gestures

Communication Style

Not surprisingly, various DISC types tend to communicate in different ways. This is where you'll most quickly be able to modify your communication to get along with others.

If you can think of someone you currently have difficulty communicating with or relating to - for example a roommate or professor, pay close attention here for what to do. If you don't know what type they are, try our speed reader, or, if you know they've taken the DISC, just ask!

> *"Tact is like a girdle – it enables you to organize the awkward truth more attractively."*

Drivers

Listen for:

~ Minimal small talk
~ Fast-paced speech
~ Direct, to-the-point communication style
~ *"Bossy"* statements and issuing orders

Types of words and phrases stereotypically used:

~ Big
~ Bottom-line
~ Stronger
~ Better
~ Results
~ Now

~ Get in or get out!
~ Lead, follow, or get out of the way
~ Things need to change around here
~ Give it to me straight
~ Let's do it now!
~ I demand...
~ We need to work harder

Influencers

Listen for:

~ Laughing
~ Telling funny stories
~ Very articulate, expressive communication style
~ Someone who tends to take over a conversation

Types of words and phrases stereotypically used:

~ Fun
~ Enthusiasm
~ Feel
~ Fantastic
~ Impressive
~ Wow!
~ Wonderful
~ Phenomenal
~ Isn't this great?
~ I'm so excited
~ Did I tell you about...?
~ Let's work together
~ Let's go!

Stabilizers

Listen for:

~ Questions about family and friends
~ A genuine interest in people
~ Concern for others
~ Someone who speaks very little in large groups

Types of words and phrases stereotypically used:

~ Nice
~ Sweet
~ Family
~ Tradition
~ Steady
~ Stable
~ Caring
~ We need to be more sensitive
~ How will this affect your family?
~ Let's take it slow
~ Let me help you
~ I'm not sure I can do that
~ What's going to happen if…?
~ How will they feel about this?

Conscientious

Listen for:

~ Slow, deliberate speaking
~ Lots of questions
~ Someone who spots inaccuracies and points them out to others
~ The one who corrects exaggerations
~ Someone with a lot of knowledge

Types of words and phrases stereotypically used:

~ Think
~ Reason
~ Analyze
~ Consider
~ Research
~ Study
~ Careful
~ Cautious
~ Investigate
~ Think about it
~ I need time to think
~ We need to be more organized

~ I don't like quick decisions
~ Figure it out
~ I don't understand; please explain
~ The intelligent thing to do is…
~ We need a back-up plan

Modifying your communication style:
Learning to communicate in a way that another type can *"hear"* is one of the most valuable ways you can use the DISC. This is like a *"cheat sheet"* to working and getting along best with everyone, including:

~ Instructors
~ Friends
~ Your family
~ Partners
~ And roommates!

When talking to a D:
Do it the direct way.

Do:
~ Be clear and specific
~ Be efficient – stick to business
~ Ask *"what"* and not *"how"* questions
~ Present facts logically and efficiently
~ Touch only on the high points of a conversation
~ Tell them the answer/result FIRST
~ Give them the bottom line
~ Remember that they get angry easily and forget just as easily

Don't:
~ Waste their time
~ Talk about irrelevant matter
~ Appear disorganized and scattered
~ Speak too slowly
~ Try small talk

When talking to an I:
Do it the fun way!

Do:

- ~ Be positive and optimistic
- ~ Look for the bright side
- ~ Ask *"who"* and not *"what"* questions
- ~ Talk about things they find interesting
- ~ Listen to their stories
- ~ Don't bog them down in details
- ~ Have a warm and friendly attitude

Don't:

- ~ Withhold information or act protective
- ~ Act as though there is all the time in the world if there isn't
- ~ Try to control the conversation or reel them in too quickly
- ~ Harp on about facts, figures, or limitations

When talking to an S:
Do it the safe way.

Do:

- ~ Start by connecting personally
- ~ Ask *"how"* and not *"what"* questions
- ~ Show interest in them as a person
- ~ Patiently draw out their opinions
- ~ Slow down
- ~ Listen attentively
- ~ Remember that they do not like confrontation and will take criticism personally!

Don't:

- ~ Rush right into business
- ~ Be impersonal or dismissive
- ~ Act possessive of information
- ~ Be overly optimistic
- ~ Be critical or confrontational

When talking to a C:
Do it the correct way.

Do:

- ~ Ask *"why"* and not *"what"* questions
- ~ Focus on step-by-step explanations
- ~ Be realistic and accurate
- ~ Prepare your *"case"* in advance
- ~ Be straightforward and business-like, especially if you don't know them well
- ~ Give them time to think things through
- ~ Provide solid proof or evidence of what you're saying
- ~ Slow down and listen carefully
- ~ If possible, sit down to talk

Don't:

- ~ Be overly bubbly or optimistic
- ~ Make claims you can't prove
- ~ Present information in a disorganized manner
- ~ Push too hard
- ~ Make unrealistic goals or promises

Group Dynamics and Teams

If you've ever wondered why some teams or groups work easily and effectively together, while others fall apart or dissolve into tension and all-out confrontation, it can often be due to the interaction of different styles in the team. If there are too many of one very pronounced style, they may overrun others or overrule the balance that other members can offer.

Flash Point!
Just like each members' individual DISC temperament, a group or team takes on a style of its own, based on the DISC types of the members. Although not everyone may individually agree with the persona that a group or team takes on, they almost always fall in line with *"the way things are done."*

Many times, by evaluating each group member's type – and the percentage of each type in a group - you can see how the team gets its outward *"personality,"* and how to best utilize the strengths of all members.

Here is a brief outline of what each type contributes to a team, and then you'll have a chance to look at the dynamics of your own group:

Drivers:
Generate ideas

What they offer:
- ~ Control
- ~ Quick decisions
- ~ Direct answers
- ~ Fast pace
- ~ Drive toward winning/achieving goals
- ~ Eagerness to tackle new challenges

As leaders, these types reward:
- ~ A go-get 'em, aggressive attitude
- ~ Decisiveness
- ~ Results
- ~ Winning / Victory
- ~ Independence

They may criticize or fail to recognize the value of:
- ~ Extensive analysis
- ~ Steady progress
- ~ Detail
- ~ Safety & Caution

Influencers
Promote ideas.

What they offer:
- ~ Social glue
- ~ Open communication – encouraging frank exchanges of view

~ Comic relief
~ Spokesperson - PR (personal and public relations)
~ Enthusiasm
~ Charisma

As leaders, these types reward:
~ Enthusiasm
~ Creativity
~ Passion
~ Optimism
~ Clever ideas
~ Autonomy

They may criticize or fail to recognize the value of:
~ Caution
~ Extensive analysis
~ Perceived insensitivity
~ An uncompromising attitude
~ Detail orientation
~ Diplomacy

Stabilizers
Support others and create detailed plans

What they offer:
~ Caution
~ Safety
~ Holding the team back from impulsive goals or hasty decisions
~ Hard work and detail
~ Stability
~ Predictability
~ Teamwork

As leaders, these types reward:
~ Loyalty
~ Cooperation
~ Teamwork

~ Thoughtfulness
~ Time spent in concern for other members
~ Punctuality

They may criticize or fail to recognize the value of:
~ A winning, aggressive attitude
~ Enthusiasm
~ Passion
~ Innovative ideas without a plan
~ Disruptions

Conscientious
Fact-checking, quality, and results.

What they offer:
~ Attention to detail
~ Quality control
~ Clarifying questions
~ An eye for spotting inconsistencies
~ Accuracy
~ Order and organization
~ Diplomacy

As leaders, these types reward:
~ Attention to detail
~ High quality
~ Accuracy
~ Dependability
~ Careful consideration, pause for thought and analysis

They may criticize or fail to recognize the value of:
~ Mistakes / Carelessness
~ Ideas without proof, plan, or research
~ Enthusiasm before the job is done
~ A go get 'em attitude

A Closer Look at Group Dynamics

For a personalized report of your group or team, you can find a DISC Group Analyzer online under the tools menu. This tool lets you build a team and see how the dynamics of various team members will work together. Maybe you have something to offer in groups that you never knew about. Maybe the quiet girl or guy is the missing key to your group or team's success. You might also find that your team is out of balance, with too many dominant types or too many people with passive behaviors.

Find out by gathering your team and trying our Group Analyzer – you can print the results when you're finished. This can be especially helpful for groups or teams that have to regularly work together to achieve something, or for groups where there is constant bickering or strife. It might be a good idea to share the results of the analysis with your coach or instructor. Here's your chance to get to the bottom of what makes your team work, or prevents it from working as well as it could!

The Moral of the Story

There are no guarantees that you'll be able to get along with everyone you meet, but there are ways to understand a little better why people behave the way they do. Knowing even a few basics and about communication styles – including your own – can help you relate to others and connect. Sometimes a slight shift in your approach - or even just the words you use - can really improve your ability to understand others, and be understood.

~ Chapter Eight ~

Kissing Frogs: Getting Along Using the PLSI

Ever wonder how you can see life so differently than your friends and family? Why have some of your friends known what they want to be since they were five years old and you STILL can't decide? Why is it that some people become best friends immediately with their roommates and others only drive each other crazy? Why is your best friend out on a date for the third time this week and you haven't met anyone in months - and where do they find the time to date, anyway? The answers to these questions have to do with their personality types. Every day, people pay big money to career counselors and psychologists to learn this valuable information about themselves. So we decided to offer it to you now, when you can really use it!

First, take the PLSI assessment to determine your personality type. The DISC assessment you've already taken is about your communication and behaviors, but the PLSI assessment is about your personality. It may help you better understand why you do what you do.

For example:
Some people recharge by spending the night in, lighting candles, and laughing at a good movie, while others want to tear up the town with a group of friends.

Within families or groups of friends, some people seem to have the ability to do everything *"right,"* while others, try as they might, never seem to live up to everyone's expectations.

All of these scenarios are usually due to little incompatibilities within personality types. Does this mean you're doomed with some people? Of course not! The key to these dilemmas is understanding each other. If you can understand where someone is coming from you can almost always reach an agreement - or at the very least, agree to disagree. By taking the time to address what is important to them (that might not be important to you), you'll be able to move a long way toward harmony.

If you haven't taken the PLSI assessment yet, it would be a good idea to take it now, before reading the rest of this chapter. Or, skip to another chapter and come back to this one when you can take the assessment.

Personality Assessment (PLSI)
If you've taken the assessment, you were given a personality type made up of four letters (for example - ESFJ, INFP, INTP), and these are a measure of some of what makes up your personality. There are sixteen type combinations, and they are made up of all of the possible combinations of four broad dimensions where human beings differ. All of the sixteen types are well represented among people. Every one of the sixteen types is valuable and capable - they are just different in a few fundamental ways.

Extrovert	*or*	**Introvert**

Sensate	*or*	**Intuitive**
Feeler	*or*	**Thinker**
Judger	*or*	**Perceiver**

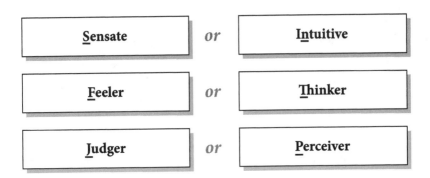

These differences represent what could be called *"traits."* These traits are something like left-handedness and right-handedness. We didn't really learn to be one or the other, and most of us did not choose one over the other. The majority of people are just dominant with one hand or the other and not usually both. And while we use both hands everyday, when we need to feel secure we tend to use our preferred hand. This is the same with each of the four dimensions. We use them all, but we usually choose our dominant preference when we need to feel comfortable.

Hopefully, just knowing your type is helpful in understanding yourself. And it may help you see how you are different from others.

The Four Personality Style Factors

EXTROVERT *(@ 60% of population)*	INTROVERT *(@ 40% of population)*
~ learns best from doing	~ likes to watch before doing
~ is more at ease & confident socially	~ prefers working alone or with one other
~ likes to know how others are doing it	~ sets own standards when possible
~ gets energized from socializing	~ likes quiet space to work
~ readily volunteers & offers opinions	~ seems *"deep"* & hard to understand
~ ideas start from the outside in	~ ideas start from inside out

SENSATE	**INTUITIVE**
(@ 65% of population)	*(@ 35% of population)*
~ is more realistic & practical	~ is more imaginative & abstract
~ is more patient & steady	~ likes new challenges, works in spurts
~ uses experience & common sense	~ trusts what makes sense to her/him
~ likes routines & order	~ dislikes routine & detail work
~ looks more for what is actual & sensible	~ looks more for what is possible
~ lives in the here & now	~ lives toward her/his vision of the future

FEELER	**THINKER**
(@ 65% females: 35% males)	*(@ 55% females: 45% males)*
~ is more interested in people than ideas	~ is more interested in fascinating ideas
~ focuses more on personal relationships	~ wants things to be fair & reasonable
~ likes harmony, dislikes conflict	~ stands up for what he/she thinks
~ is tuned in to others' feelings	~ is tuned in to logical consistency
~ is warm & arouses enthusiasm	~ is cool-headed & impartial in conflict
~ makes decisions based on his/her heart	~ makes decisions based on rational thought

JUDGER	**PERCEIVER**
(@ 45% of population)	*(@ 55% of population)*
~ is more decisive than curious	~ is more curious than decisive
~ likes planned & scheduled activities	~ likes the spontaneous & unplanned
~ has very set opinions	~ is flexible, adaptable, & tolerant
~ feels good when things are completed	~ likes to keep options open
~ likes order & organization	~ seeks more to understand than to manage
~ may make decisions too quickly	~ may have trouble making up her/his mind

The combination of your four preferences makes up your *"personality style."* Taking the underlined letters from the titles above, you'll end up with one of the sixteen possible combinations (for example - ENTJ, ISFP, ESTP, or INFJ). Remember there are definitely no *"better"* or *"more important"* styles. It takes all types to make the world go 'round!

The more your score falls on one side of the column than the other, the easier it will be for you to use those traits or ways of thinking. This is why you may find that some people are harder to understand than others. Just like consciously shifting to your less dominant hand when performing simple daily tasks, being able to understand and relate to others may require you to shift into a way of thinking you don't use very often.

Notice that if you score only slightly into the left or right of a column, but are more near the center, you may find it relatively easy to try a different way of thinking. For example, it might not be very hard to use a different hand to pour your shampoo in the morning, or to use a different hand to eat. The further your score falls on once side of the column than the other, the harder it may be for you to operate in a different way. Think about throwing a baseball with a different hand, or surfing with your *"other"* foot forward, and you can imagine how hard you'll sometimes have to try to understand another person's way of thinking.

While we all have the ability to use traits on both sides of each column, understanding the traits that are the most comfortable for you will help you learn to be more successful and appreciate your unique gifts. You can learn more about how your preferences affect your style of learning, living and acting in the following pages.

Type Dimension Comparison

Extroversion		**Introversion**
Immersion into action	**Energy from**	Peaceful withdrawal
Doing first	**Learn from**	Watching first
Initiate the interaction	**Interaction**	Wait to be approached
In groups	**Socializing**	Series of one on ones
Externally expressive	**Expression**	Externally reserved
Outside/Accommodating	**Thinking**	Inside/Autonomous

Sensate		Intuitive
Practical reality	**World**	Socially constructed
Respect for what is	**Reality**	Imagine what could be
Present	**Time orientation**	Future
Experience	**Effectiveness comes from**	Ingenuity
What works	**Data for tasks**	What makes sense

Feeling		Thinking
People	**Basic value**	Rational
Wholes/Similarities	**Looking at things**	Patterns/Differences
Resist it	**Approach to conflict**	Invigorated by it
Warm and readable	**Affect**	Cool and reserved
Praise and encouragement	**Motivation**	Achievement and goals

Judging		Perceiving
Decisive	**Decision style**	Open-minded
Convergent	**Approach to information**	Divergent
Linear/Sequential	**Cognitive pattern**	Random/Circular
Clock time is valid	**Time**	General/Flexible
Completion	**Comfort in tasks**	Getting started

If you know the four letter type of someone, reading this comparison chart can help you understand more about where they may be coming from. Unlike DISC, it isn't always possible to *"speed read"* a person's personality type so easily. Being able to determine someone else's PLSI type is very difficult without seeing their actual scores. Someone may appear to you to be an obvious extrovert, for example, because they are gregarious and bubbly, always ready for conversation, or they're very funny in class. However, the reality is that they may do most of their thinking on their own, not necessarily needing to run things by others, or they may recharge by time alone (peaceful withdrawal) instead of talking to friends or engaging in physical activity (immersion into action). They may actually be an introvert after all! Remember, we all have the ability to use both traits.

	Extroverts (E)	Introverts (I)
Sensates (S)	**ES's: Action-oriented Realists** *(@ 40% of population)* This type loves action and things happening. They like to get practical results from their work and like to work in groups. For them, too much watching is a waste of time. They want to do. They like to share what they are doing and thinking. They get impatient when things are too slow, complicated, or abstract.	**IS's: Thoughtful Realists** *(@ 25% of population)* This type is the most careful and steady. They don't mind working alone or with one other. They like practical results and are good with details and technical things. They are often the least expressive; they see much but usually share little. They don't like careless ideas, plans, or too many new things at once.
Intuitives (N)	**EN's: Action-oriented Innovators** *(@ 25% of population)* This type is really motivated and likes to make things happen. They like to work in groups on new and interesting things. They like to take their theories and apply them with others. They share easily, especially what's inside. They don't like details, routines, or the same old thing for too long.	**IN's: Thoughtful Innovators** *(@ 10% of population)* This type is the best at solving problems. They like to work at their own pace on their own ideas. They like to make creative and scientific things. They would rather express themselves through their thoughts instead of socializing with lots of others. They don't like doing busy work or things that don't make sense.

Looking at this chart, you might begin to see how your type could affect your study methods.

For example:
ES's and EN's would work well in a group study situation. Both of these types like a fast-moving environment where they can get through a lot of material. Both of these types may also need to work a little bit harder to focus on listening, because they may have a tendency to do all the talking when in a group.

IS's and IN's are probably at their best studying alone, where they can concentrate. This isn't to say that these types wouldn't benefit from being in a study group – it's just that they will probably get their overview of a subject by studying alone, and then check themselves against what others might think at a study group.

Sensates	**SP's: Sensible, Adaptable, Active types** *(@ 33% of population)* When sensate qualities are combined with perceiver qualities the result is usually someone very tuned in to the here and now. They like doing and playing today, and not being too worried about tomorrow. They are the most spontaneous and easy-going. They like to get involved in new and interesting activities. School can be boring for the SP if it means sitting still and doing all written work, but it can be fun too because that's often where the action is.	**SJ's: Sensible, Decision-making types** *(@ 30% of population)* When sensate qualities are combined with judging qualities the result is usually someone who is very dependable and responsible. The SJ type is very service-oriented and they are good *"team players"*. They most like situations that are spelled out and well-organized. SJ's like institutions such as school, teams, church and family. They usually don't mind step-by-step work, and they like and perform well in school (partly because most teachers are SJ's themselves).
Intuitives	**NF's: Enthusiastic, Insightful types** (@ 22% of population) When intuition is combined with feeling qualities, the result is someone who is very good with people and language. The NF is usually very enthusiastic and warm. They are very oriented toward cooperative things and away from competitive things. They usually have very strong feelings about things and people; they really like them or really don't. NF's are very personal types and thrive in supportive, creative, and harmonious situations.	**NT's: Logical, Ingenious types** *(@ 15% of population)* When intuition is combined with a thinking style the result is someone who always needs to know *"why?"* NT's are less interested in how things have been done, and more interested in how they can improve and change them. They are very imaginative and are very comfortable in the *"world of ideas."* They like to be good at things and always want to be learning. They can appear unemotional, and can be accused of having an *"attitude,"* which is usually not the case.

You and your roommate

Whether you are living with someone of your choosing, or have been paired with a roommate in your dorm, it can certainly be difficult to get along at times. If your roommate is willing, try exchanging your detailed result to the personality assessment (PLSI). The first overview report is good for you to learn about yourself, but the second, more detailed report is helpful for how you relate to others - and how others can relate to you.

One area for roommates in particular to watch for is J-P: judgers and perceivers. Judgers are more likely to enjoy an ordered, organized environment. They don't tend to like interruptions. Perceivers, on the other hand, may tend to be less tidy. They often have no problem at all with interruptions - in fact, they sometimes thrive on them! You can imagine how this can cause problems when a judger and a perceiver live together; they tend not to agree on their environment, who does what chores, and why so many chores are necessary in the first place. To the judger, it's obvious that things need to be done. To the perceiver, those obvious things may not even register.

When it comes to studying, judgers may require uninterrupted time, and perceivers may feel stifled by the quiet and the *"rules."*

Extroverts and introverts paired together can sometimes have a hard time communicating. For the extrovert who just wants to talk and enjoy their roommate, the introvert's need for privacy can feel hurtful. To the introvert who just needs time to recharge, the extrovert's attempts at talk can feel invasive or even annoying.

Finally, there can be examples of pairs - especially when there are many opposing preferences - where one roommate is very controlling, and the other may not be assertive enough to set their own boundaries, which can be stressful. Likewise, two very assertive roommates together can drive each other crazy, by each wanting things their own way.

Flash Point!
You can imagine how talking about these differences, or at the very least thinking about them, may help you to come up with a compromise. You have everything to gain by working together - tension at home or in your dorm room can affect your studies and grades, as well as how much fun you have in college.

With friends and partners
Here is another great opportunity to exchange detailed personality assessment results to learn about those you love. Is one of you an introvert, and one an extrovert? If so, you might frequently have trouble deciding what to do for fun. The extrovert might feel frustrated at the lack of social time needed by the introvert. The introvert can feel pressured to do things in the name of fun that they genuinely don't consider fun!

If you're a J-P combination, the perceiver may drive the judger crazy with their apparent inability to make quick decisions. Likewise, perceivers may think judgers act too quickly without exploring all possibilities.

To a feeling type, a thinking type can seem cold and uncaring. To the thinking type, a feeler can seem illogical. On the other hand, this combination can offer great opportunities for learning and growth.

Sensing and intuitive types can make excellent teams, each being interested in the parts of work the other doesn't like so much. But they can also have a hard time seeing eye-to-eye. These types can also help each other grow, and have plenty to teach each other.

Learning about those around you can really improve your relationships. It can also provide you with a mirror to learn more about yourself. Give it a try!

When you're under pressure
Understanding personality types will help you throughout your life in any

team environment, in relationships with your co-workers, bosses and employees, and in your personal relationships.

Flash Point!
When you're under pressure, depending on your personality type, you may react in ways that aren't normal for you. This might be when you're sick or really stressed out about an exam, for example. If you're overly tired, you might find you're not yourself, either. Finally, sometimes just being in a close situation with someone of an opposite type will cause you to exhibit signs of strain.

Take a look at your PLSI results, and how your personality type reacts under pressure. Can you identify ways this may have affected your attitude and perspective at times? What about with your roommate, or friends?

For example, when under extreme pressure or stress, INFJ's and INTJ's often develop an adversarial attitude, making them feel that no one can help them. This feeling of *"doom and gloom"* can greatly affect their attitude.

When ENTJ's and ESFJ's are under pressure, they can become self-critical. When in this state of mind, they cling to unreasonable assumptions about themselves, *"I'm not smart enough to finish school," "I'll never learn this stuff."* Often the trigger for these times is feeling misunderstood by others. If there is too much conflict, and not enough harmony in their lives, these types will react negatively toward themselves.

Your type and studying
Of course, knowing your type can help you determine the best ways to study, but it may also help you gain an understanding of how you process information – what your mind focuses on, and how it finds meaning. Once you know that, you can find more effective study methods.

If you're an introvert, and you find study groups intimidating and exhausting, don't keep trying to attend because you feel you *"should,"* or because a close friend finds them helpful.

Or, let's say that – even being an introvert – you have always enjoyed study groups, but have recently found them annoying. This is not a reason to write off study groups forever. Upon reflection, you may find that during times of stress you go further inside yourself, making them just too social an environment. You'll probably enjoy them again when pressure has eased.

As a sensing type, your mind focuses on facts and practicality. You look to gather relevant, specific data. You learn new information in a step-by-step, practical manner. You'll work well with lists and outlines because of the way you organize information.

On the other hand, an intuitive type focuses on patterns and meanings. You like to generate your own alternative interpretations of factual data. You learn new information insight by insight, in a theoretical manner. You'll work well with mind maps and cards that you can move into groups because of the way you look for and organize information.

Does this mean that a sensing type shouldn't use mind maps, or an intuitive type won't find an outline useful? Not at all! It's just helpful to know your most natural tendencies.

Knowing your personality and learning types may also help you find effective study partners. A sensing type studying with an intuitive type may find the intuitive to be too unfocused, and the intuitive might find the sensing type too exhaustive!

Your type and your career

Your personality type can play a big role in what you might like to do for work, and consequently the major you choose.

ISTJ

Careers: Management, Administration, Law Enforcement, Accounting

Or any other occupations where they can use their experience, attention to detail and dedication to organizational goals to accomplish practical tasks.

ISFJ

Careers: Education, Health Care, Religious Settings

Or any other occupations where they can use their experience and/or their understanding of organizational standards to help others and support the *"team."*

INFJ

Careers: Religion, Counseling, Teaching, Arts, Writing

Or any other occupations where they can facilitate the emotional, intellectual and spiritual development of others and/or express their ideas in writing and plans.

INTJ

Careers: Science, Computers, Law, Academics

Or any other occupations where they can use their intellectual creativity to create plans and schemes and/or their ease with technology to solve problems.

ISTP

Careers: Skilled Trades, Technical Fields, Computers, Agriculture, Military

Or any other occupations where they can use their practical expertise to solve technical problems and/or process information effectively.

ISFP

Careers: Health Care, Business, Law Enforcement

Or any other occupations where they can use their attention to detail in a service-oriented field.

INFP

Careers: Counseling, Writing, Arts

Or any other occupations where they can use their creativity in independent ways and/or where they feel the freedom to grow.

INTP

Careers: Sciences, Technical Fields, Computers, Design

Or any other occupations where they can use their analytical ability in independent ways to solve problems, invent and discover.

ESTP

Careers: Marketing, Skilled Trades, Business, Law Enforcement, Applied Technology

Or any other occupations where they can use their *"doer"* nature to find technical solutions and make sure practical work is carried out successfully.

ESFP

Careers: Health Care, Coaching, Skilled Trades, Childcare, Public Relations

Or any other occupations where they can use their outgoing nature and people skills to help people with their practical needs.

ENFP

Careers: Counseling, Teaching, Religion, Arts, Public Relations

Or any other occupations where they can use their energy and people skills to motivate and help groups and individuals grow and/or work together better.

ENTP

Careers: Science, Management, Technology, Arts, Design

Or any other occupations where they can use their analytical skills and multiple talents to help groups function more effectively and solve new challenges.

ESTJ

Careers: Management, Administration, Law Enforcement

Or any other occupations where they can use their organizational and leadership skills to help others execute the task in the most efficient manner.

ESFJ

Careers: Education, Health Care, Religion

Or any other occupations where they can use their instinct for teaching and caring for others; with a primary focus on practical needs and creating harmonious organizations.

ENFJ

Careers: Education, Religion, Social Work, Arts

Or any other occupations where they can use their people skills and enthusiasm to help others grow, make meaning of and understand the big picture.

ENTJ

Careers: Management, Law, Leadership, Technology

Or any other occupations where they can use their natural leadership skills and analytical ability to help organize and marshal the energy needed to get collective tasks done.

One of the type variances that may affect your choice of career is whether you are more of a thinking type, or a feeling type. For example, notice how most counselors and teachers are feeling types as opposed to thinking types on the list of occupational trends graphics. This wouldn't mean you need to reconsider your choice if you're a thinking type planning to teach, but it does indicate a general preference that most, but not all teachers tend to be feeling types. It's a good idea to think about why that might be, and whether that reason will affect you in your work.

Something else to consider is whether you are an introvert or an extrovert. Although many introverts are successful in occupations where they are required to spend a lot of time working with others (as opposed to working on their own), this may take a lot more energy for them than it would for an extrovert.

This is just something to note, and it doesn't mean that you can't be happy in any career you choose. If you have taken the Work Importance assessment, you'll already have given some thought to what is important to you. The Career Interests assessment will also have helped you narrow down what you are truly interested in.

Your Type in a Group

If you're in a group or team, and especially if you are a leader, it can help to know the types of other members of the group. If possible, have everyone bring their detailed personality assessment (PLSI) report when you meet. This will give you insight into their personalities and how they might react to various leadership styles. You may also want to have a group discussion to identify the temperament needs of each of the individuals. This will help you all perform better together in the long run.

Leadership and personality

Understanding your type can be very useful in understanding and developing your leadership style.

For each of the four type combinations, vision is typically based on:

ES Shared tasks and experience
IS Tasks and accomplishments
EN Shared principals and action
IN An internal interpretation of the big picture

For each of the four type combinations, priorities can be very different:

SF People's feelings and getting practical needs met
ST Consistency and practical realities
NF Meaningful outcomes and emotional harmony
NT Logical consistency and relevancy

Communication: A good leader needs to be able to develop a vision of the goals of the group, and then communicate that vision with clarity. You can see how you might need to touch on different aspects of your vision for an SF than you would an NF. Considering everybody's needs can help you address all concerns.

Decision Making: A good leader considers the will of the group and other information before making a decision. If members of your group have different priorities, you'll have to allow for them when making a decision.

Shared Values: An effective leader knows that unless the group feels comfortable with the vision and decisions of the group and the leader, harmony will not last and the group will suffer.

Every type is valuable and every type has something to offer. So whether it's you and your roommate, you and your baseball team, or you and your partner or spouse, taking time to explore your personality assessment results will help you bring out the best in each other, and achieve success in whatever way is important to you.

The Moral of the Story

Your personality type strongly influences the way you feel and your reasons for doing what you do. If you've ever marveled at how different you are from certain family members or friends, the mystery is solved here! When you take our personality assessment (PLSI) you'll gain insight into your own personality type, and if you share your report with others, they may start to understand you a little better, too. If you're having a hard time with a parent or roommate or are a leader of a large group, take time to step outside of yourself and address what might be important to others – even if it's not important to you. Sometimes a little understanding goes a long way.

~ Chapter Nine ~
Managing Your Pot of Gold

Not having enough money is one of the most frequently named reasons for college failure. However, the good news is that with good budgeting and a little sacrifice, money problems - including a lack of funds - can be overcome. Careful planning may need to happen, but the sacrifice is worth it: overall, college graduates are paid more than non-grads, and generally get their pick of better jobs. Once you finish college, it won't take long to make up for lost time financially, and you'll probably like your job a lot more.

Future jobs, and the promise of more money in a few years might not mean much to you when you're living on frozen burritos and ramen noodles *because it's all you can afford.* This is where some of the goal setting discipline you learned in earlier chapters will serve you well! And the information that follows will help you get through these tough years.

Even if you're doing ok on the money front, many college students tell us that they didn't learn basic money management skills in school. Things like how credit ratings work, and how to pick the best health insurance for your lifestyle. If you've ever wondered what's so important about compound interest, you'll soon see! We'll try to answer all of your money questions about banking, credit cards, cars, budgeting, saving and plenty more.

Testing your money savvy
Campus ToolKit has a Financial Awareness quiz online that will help you pinpoint the areas you need help with, and relax when it comes to areas you really do know. All of the answers are in this chapter, so look here when you have a money question on the assessment that stumps you.

Spending money

Bank Accounts
A bank account is necessary for most college students. If you qualify for financial aid, you may need a place to put your quarterly or semester payments so that you'll have access to cash whenever you need it. Similarly, if you receive money from your family, you'll need a safe way to deposit the money and use only what you need. Finally, if you have a part-time job, you'll need a place to cash your checks.

You may already have a savings or checking account. Bank accounts are a good tool – they help you budget, and are a great alternative to keeping money stuffed under your mattress … it's one of the first places a thief will look!

Here is a quick run-down of the most common bank accounts you'll encounter:

Checking Account
This is an account that allows you to draw money from your balance (the amount in your account) by check. You deposit money in, and the money is there for you to withdraw, whether that is by an ATM, debit card, or writing checks.

Checking accounts are the most popular form of bank account, and offer a lot of convenience. Normally there is a monthly fee and/or a minimum balance required for a checking account. In certain accounts, the fee will be lower or waived if you can keep a minimum balance in the account at all times - but usually the balance required is somewhere between $500 and $1000 - not easy in college!

Shop around for the best rate, and look for a bank that has a location near you. Sometimes it's helpful to bank with a major bank, so that you'll find a branch wherever you go. If you receive an allowance, this means your parents can place money in the account at a branch near their home, and you can withdraw money at a branch near you. Alternatively, you may find that you appreciate the personal service you get at a smaller bank.

Paying by Check

Checks are especially convenient for paying bills, since cash shouldn't be sent through the mail. They can also act as a receipt for payment, because your bank can tell you if the check has been cashed, and trace the account number of the person who cashed it. There is usually a small fee for this service.

If you mail a check and someone says they didn't receive it, just ask your bank if it has been cashed. If it hasn't, you can write the person a new check, and cancel the lost check. This is called putting a *"stop payment"* on the check. If anyone ever tries to present the check again, it will not be cashed. Do this only when necessary, because banks almost always charge a fee for stopped checks.

Bounced Checks

Be careful when writing checks. If enough money isn't in your bank account to cover a check you've written, the check will be returned to the person you were paying marked *"NSF," "Non-Sufficient Funds"* or *"Insufficient Funds."*

Flash Point!
Writing checks without funds is commonly known as *"bouncing checks,"* and is bad financial management. It results in a black mark on your credit rating, and will usually make the person who tried to cash the check really mad. Not only will they be annoyed, but they may be reluctant to take a check from you in the future. Your bank will charge you a fee for having insufficient funds, and the person who tried to cash the check will be charged a fee by their bank, which you'll have to pay...it's only fair.

If you do this more than once, you may find that your checks will no longer be accepted in locations where checks are processed through a check guarantee service – which is most grocery stores and major retailers.

Finally, checks are not a form of credit, or a way to buy time. If you write a check thinking it will take a few days for the check to clear, and you know you'll have money in the account by then, you're eventually going to get caught. If the person the check is written to happens to bank at the same bank you do, it will clear your account that very night. Also, some retailers verify with your bank that funds are available before they accept a check, and if they aren't there, it can be very embarrassing. The retailer will presume you were trying to bounce a check. Not cool.

I didn't mean it ... *honest*!
Sometimes you can bounce a check by accident, because you're not keeping track of how much money is in your account. A lot can be happening in a checking account: Bank fees go through unannounced, fees for checkbooks, checks you've written, ATM and bank withdrawals going out, and money coming in. Add to that any direct debits or electronic payments, and it's pretty easy to be in the dark about how much money is in the account.

To avoid this, get in the habit of writing down the check number and dollar amount of checks written in your checkbook, along with all other transactions like ATM withdrawals and money going in. This is keeping a checkbook journal. Most checkbooks come with one for you to use. If yours doesn't, ask your bank for one.

Balancing your checkbook

If you are keeping track of these transactions, it should be very easy to balance your checkbook regularly. Balancing your checkbook simply means matching your records to the bank's records. In other words, making sure your balance is the same as what the bank says, by checking each transaction.

Balancing your checkbook should be done a minimum of once a month, when your statement comes. If there is any discrepancy, the details will be fresh in your mind if you're balancing regularly. Discrepancies include things like:

- An ATM withdrawal you forgot to record.
- Your bank losing one of your deposits.
- An electronic payment being repeated twice.
- Bank fees automatically hitting your account that you knew nothing about.

Here's how to balance your checkbook:

1. Start with either a printed bank statement, or a statement that you've printed online or at an ATM.
2. Compare your balances.
   Are they the same? If so, great. Your balance matches theirs, and you can go on about your day. This doesn't happen very often, because usually a few days have passed since the statement was printed, and transactions could have taken place since then.
3. If your balance doesn't match the bank, you need to find the transaction or transactions that don't match.
   - Is there something on the bank statement that isn't in your checkbook journal? An example would be bank fees, or an ATM withdrawal you forgot about.
   - Is there something in your checkbook journal that isn't on the statement? An example would be checks you wrote that haven't cleared the bank yet, or a deposit you made after they printed and mailed the statement.

If you don't see it right away,

- ~ Run through the transactions on the statement and in your journal, ticking off each one that matches on both the journal and the statement.
- ~ Don't forget to check the dollar amounts, in case you wrote the wrong amount in your journal, or the bank amount is incorrect.
- ~ When you're finished, find the transactions that don't have a match, or are a different amount: they're the problem - fix them, and you're done.

4. Hey, still can't find it? Sometimes, if you have a lot of transactions, it's hard to find the discrepancy.
   - ~ Try calculating the difference between your bank balance and your checkbook balance and looking for exactly that amount.
   - ~ Next, try doubling or halving the difference and looking for that amount.
   - ~ Check the dates of the statement – is your statement missing a period of time?

Just keep looking for the difference, and you'll find the problem.

ATM and Check Cards/Debit Cards

These are cards issued by your bank that allow you to withdraw funds without having to go to the bank. An ATM (Automated Teller Machine) card lets you get money from cash machines.

A check or debit card can be used like an ATM card, but it can also be used like a check where credit cards are accepted. You'll be asked for your PIN (a secret code that only you should know). *If you've got the money in your account, it's taken right then just like a check.* If you don't have the money to cover the transaction, it will be declined. An advantage is that it also looks and acts like a credit card, so you can order things online and through catalogs with most debit cards.

Remember: When you use a check card, be sure to record the transaction in your check register.

Bank Fees

ATM Fees and Debit/Check Card Fees

Banks can be very creative when it comes to charging fees. Most banks charge a monthly fee for having an account. The account fee varies from bank to bank, depending on what services are included and the type of account. Other classic fee-charging opportunities are: a fee for every check that clears the bank, a fee for every withdrawal, and a fee for approaching the counter and taking a human bank-teller's time - for a transaction that could have been handled at an ATM.

The bottom line with bank fees is; be savvy, shop around, and read the fine print. It's your responsibility to know what fees your bank charges.

By the way, be aware of using your ATM or debit card in places other than your bank. Sometimes the bank whose ATM you are using will charge you a fee – usually they inform you of it at the time of the transaction. Avoid free-standing machines that you might find in convenience stores and shopping malls – they sometimes charge an even higher fee.

Online Banking

Many banks offer online banking these days, and it can be very useful. It's a way to check your account balance up to the minute, and often you can do nifty things like pay bills and transfer money between your accounts. If you don't have online banking already, ask your bank about what they can offer, and what it will cost you to use.

PayPal

With more and more transactions taking place online, PayPal has become a very popular and easy way to send and receive money.

The way it works:

Sending Money: Sending money through PayPal is free for the sender. You can send money from a credit card, debit card, or from your own PayPal account (if funds are available).

Receiving Money: Receiving money through PayPal incurs a fee, and the fee varies. To receive money through PayPal you must have an account – personal accounts are free to set up. PayPal makes their money by taking a fee from the payment being transferred into an account. For example, if you are receiving $500 into your PayPal account, a percentage of the $500 will be taken and the remainder will be transferred into your account.

Once money has been paid into your PayPal account (and PayPal has taken its fee), you can choose to leave it in your Paypal account so you can make purchases with it, or draw the money down to a bank account. There is no fee for drawing money down to a bank account, or for sending money from your account for any reason.

Always ensure that both the sender and receiver know about the fees to avoid any surprises. For example, if you send $500 through PayPal, the receiver may be expecting a full $500 – not $500 less a fee!

Budgeting for expenses

Savings Account

You can also get a savings account at your bank. Often a savings account doesn't offer you as many ways to withdraw your money as a checking account, but they may cost less. Banks may charge a small fee when you need to remove money, so ask before opening an account.

These accounts are mostly for holding money – like money put aside for car repairs or bills you'll have to pay later – that you don't want to have in your checking account. That's why, when it comes to budgeting, savings accounts can be really helpful.

So, what is budgeting?

Budgeting is a way of knowing what you're spending, and what you've got to spend. It's that simple. It's a great idea to do a budget every time you have a big change in either income or expenses – like getting a new job, or financing a car.

For most college students, constant budgeting is required just to get by and not run out of money on a regular basis. Whether attending directly from high school or as a returning student, college students don't usually have a lot of extra cash. That means you'll have to keep a close eye on your budget.

Flash Point!
Why should I do a budget, anyway?
Having a budget and sticking to it is a way for you to live within your means. In other words, living comfortably with the amount of money you have - and not spending what you don't have. Although that might not sound fun, the reality is that you'll feel better and have less worries when you do. When you're in college, *"less worries"* are a whole lot better than a new jacket or a weekend away.

What goes into a budget?
EVERYTHING. Don't forget annual expenses: things like car tags, books, and travel plans for the summer all have to be budgeted for. There are some sneaky expenses to remember, too, like deposits you'll need for renting an apartment, and regular maintenance on your car.

What's so hard about budgeting?
The more frequently your money comes in, the easier it is to stick to your budget. Weekly is pretty easy – even if you blow it, you only have a few days to wait until more cash comes in. Every other week is still pretty good: in fact, every two weeks is how the majority of people get paid. If your money comes only once a month, it can be a bit harder to plan. If you receive most of your income quarterly or twice a year - like from financial aid - budgeting gets even more important … *and more difficult.*

Retail Therapy
Sometimes, when you take money and put it aside for use over the following few weeks, it just doesn't stop tempting you! The little voice inside of your head keeps saying, *"Get the new bag – you need it for school." "The shoes you wanted are on sale – you can't pass this up!" "You deserve it – you've been working so hard!"* This is what is known as retail therapy: spending with abandon and no thought of things like how you're going to eat.

The emotional lift that comes from retail therapy is short lived. Actually, *"short lived"* is an understatement. The come-down can be stressful – or even downright depressing! On items like shoes and clothing, the buzz is often gone after the first wear. Bummer.

Sometimes waiting actually feels better!

Here's a formula you were never taught in math class:

Retail Therapy = Financial Drama

You didn't really have the money, but you spent it. Now you don't have any money, and you need it. You felt great while you were spending money, but now you feel bad – totally broke and maybe a little bit queasy.

Instead of dealing with these ups and downs, another option is to wait until you actually have the money to buy something. It leaves you feeling empowered and in control of your life. Retail therapy is a little bit like stealing from yourself. Waiting until you can afford something rewards yourself, and it feels fantastic!

Saving for Unexpected Expenses

If you can think of it, it has to be budgeted for - but what about things you could never see coming? Needing a new set of tires on your car, or getting a parking ticket? What about getting sick, and not being able to work for a day or two? That's where saving money comes in – we briefly talked about it earlier in this chapter in the banking section.

Planning and saving for unexpected expenses is hard. There is no warning when these expenses are coming, and no guarantee that they'll show up at all! So do you really want to take $20 and put it away for something that may or may not happen, or would you rather go out for a night on the town, or treat yourself to a nice lunch? One is infinitely more attractive than the other, but ...

Simply put, saving money is how you put distance between you, and poverty. Not having enough money is stressful. In college, you have enough to think about, without adding money worries. So put a little aside and live free!

How do I know what my budget is?

There are only two sides to a budget: Money coming in, and money going out.

Below is an example budget. This person has it pretty sweet; they don't have to pay rent or a car payment, they get a monthly allowance, and their Mom buys them new clothes every time she comes to visit. Take a look:

Budget Example

Item	Income (in)	Expense (out)
Monthly Allowance	$ 500.00	
Grocery Store Food *(monthly)*		$ 200.00
Gas for the car *(monthly)*		$ 80.00
Lunches out *(monthly)*		$ 90.00
One afternoon a week tutoring	$ 40.00	
Weekend Fun-Money *($20 a weekend)*		$ 80.00
Wednesday night at the movies *(4x)*		$ 40.00
Savings		$ 20.00
Totals:	**$ 540.00**	**$ 510.00**
Leftover spending money:	*$ 30.00*	

This person has thirty bucks leftover! Not all of us are so lucky. But where do you stand?

Budgeting Tool

Campus ToolKit has a nifty budgeting tool online where you can enter your actual expenses and income, and see a completely personalized working budget. It's also an easy way to experiment with your budget to see where you can cut costs that might result in more fun money.

Making a little extra money

A part-time job can be fun, and the extra cash goes a long way toward your finances. Just make sure the job doesn't interfere with school – you may need all the time you can get for studying when you have a heavy class schedule. It's important to be able to have some time off, too, so don't create a different kind of stress for yourself by taking on too much.

Cars

We give cars a mention in the money chapter because they cost so much. They're hard to budget for, because they're riddled with extra, hidden costs. So, pay careful attention to car costs when you do your budgeting, and when you consider your next car purchase.

Hidden Costs

When you think of how much a car will cost you, what comes to mind? Probably the payment (if you're financing) and the cost if you're buying it outright. Gas, of course. And insurance.

From here, it gets murky. Things you only have to pay once a year, for example car tags and car maintenance, tend to be written off to the *"deal with later"* section of our consciousness. BUT, forgetting about the expenses doesn't mean they'll go away. In fact, it's so easy to save for these types of expenses if you budget for them and save a tiny bit each week. It's a lot easier to stick away $11 a week than come up with $550 all at once if your car breaks down, or car tags are due.

How to expect the unexpected

Because it's hard to calculate yearly expenses, or anticipate car repairs that may or may not happen, we've dedicated a whole section of our online Money Management module to help you with car expenses. Check it out for answers to all of your questions.

Owning your dream car

One final word about cars: Many of us spend a lot of time thinking about what it would be like to own a really nice car ...

... But your time in college is not the time to own your dream car.

Flash Point!

Getting through college is expensive, and many students who have high car payments find they can't afford to stay in school. Sacrificing your college career - for a car - is extremely short-sighted.

Even if you manage to pay big car payments while you're in school, it often takes all the money you could be having fun with!

By waiting just a bit longer until you graduate from college and get your first well-paid job, you'll be able to actually *afford* a nice car. Then you can be the one with the college degree, working at what you love, driving *whatever car you want.*

Until then, stay focused on getting ahead, and drive something cheap and functional. Besides, it's a lot more fun to spend your Sunday afternoon driving your friends to the beach in a 1981 beater than working extra hours at a part-time job to pay for your nice car.

Saving Money

Before we even start talking about saving money, let's just lay the truth on the table: Saving money is hard, and nobody wants to do it. Anytime you are faced with the decision to take some of your money and put it aside for "*savings,*" it's certainly not as fun as the idea of taking that money and buying something you want!

The fact is saving money is how you get what you want. It's one of the primary skills you will need for a successful future.

How to save easily

Saving is more of a habit than anything. Decide what you want, whether it's a new pair of jeans, a ski trip, a down payment on a house or independent wealth, and figure out what you'll need to save to get it.

Reasons to save

There are three very distinct and separate reasons for saving money:

1. **Saving for something specific**

   Most of us have experience with this type of saving. When you don't have enough money for something that you want, you save for it - a little at a time. For small things, you may only need to save for a week or so – by watching what you spend and putting as much money aside as possible.

If it's something bigger, like a backpacking trip to Europe next year or a car, you may need a simple savings plan so that you know what to save from now until then. Figure out what the trip is going to cost, count the weeks or months until then, and calculate how much you'll have to regularly put aside to have what you need.

This type of saving is the way you'll have money for expenses you know are coming up – like car insurance or a big night out for a friend's birthday.

2. Saving for unexpected expenses

This is what is often referred to as *"saving for a rainy day."* Certain situations are going to come up – like your car needing new tires, or getting the flu and not being able to work your part time job for a week – but you may not know when or how.

Having money put aside for unexpected expenses results in a lot less stress in your life. If you have enough money for whatever can come up, you don't have anything to worry about. When something needs to be paid that you don't have the money for, it makes life very stressful.

After completing the budgeting section, you'll have a better idea of unexpected expenses and how to save for them.

3. Saving for life

Consider this puzzle:

"I give you a large piece of paper, and I ask you to fold it over once, and then take that folded paper and fold it over again, and then again, and again, until you have refolded the original paper 50 times. How tall do you think the final stack is going to be? In answer to that question, most people will fold the sheet in their mind's eye, and guess that the pile would be as thick as a phone book or, if they're really courageous, they'll say that it would be as tall as a refrigerator. But the real answer is that the height of the stack would approximate the distance to the sun. And if you folded it over one more time, the stack would be as high as the distance to the sun and back."

This interesting snippet comes from Malcolm Gladwell's book The Tipping Point, and it illustrates how regular saving habits can build incredible wealth over a lifetime.

Flash Point!
When you are in your early twenties, you're in a unique and enviable position for saving. It is possible for you to regularly put aside a small percentage of your income, and turn that saving into serious wealth. You have one shot at this, and with each year that passes, your position weakens.

What we're talking about is the *"miracle"* of compound interest. If you want to see how, just by saving 15% of your income (based on an average college graduate's income) starting when you're 22 you could end up with over FIFTEEN MILLION DOLLARS after 55 years, check out the charts below. They demonstrate the surprising amount of wealth you could accumulate by saving!

The following charts show how compound interest works if you save 15% of your income every year. The chart is based on the average entry-level income of college grads in the United States, assuming your wages will increase 4% a year. It also assumes a 10% rate of return, which means that your money earns 10% a year in interest. The huge differences you see in the three charts are a result of how long you are able to save.

An example of what saving 15% of your income at a 10% rate of return assuming an annual increase in wages of 4% will be worth after 55 years can be seen on the following page:

Year	Age	Income	Deposit (15% of income)	Interest	Total Value of Investment
1	22	$ 30,337.00	$ 4,550.55	$ 455.05	$ 5,005.60
5	26	$ 35,490.00	$ 5,323.50	$ 2,987.11	$ 32,858.22
10	31	$ 43,179.01	$ 6,476.85	$ 8,445.05	$ 92,895.53
20	41	$ 63,915.48	$ 9,587.32	$ 34,405.02	$ 378,455.17
25	46	$ 77,762.96	$ 11,644.44	$ 61,954.75	$ 681,502.24
30	51	$ 94,610.53	$ 14,191.58	$ 107,741.89	$ 1,185,160.81
35	56	$ 115,108.17	$ 17,266.23	$ 183,207.78	$ 2,015,285.59
40	61	$ 140,046.69	$ 21,007.00	$ 306,845.37	$ 3,375,299.05
45	66	$ 170,388.22	$ 25,558.23	$ 508,518.71	$ 5,593,705.86
50	71	$ 207,303.32	$ 31,095.50	$ 836,422.71	$ 9,200,649.84
55	76	$ 252,216.19	$ 37,832.43	$ 1,368,295.59	**$ 15,051,251.52**

In 55 years, the value of this fifteen millions dollars is approximately equal to $2,961,000.00 in today's dollars (assuming 3% annual inflation).

Let's see how much you would get if you waited ten years and started saving at 31 years old ...

Year	Age	Income	Deposit (15% of income)	Interest	Total Value of Investment
1	31	$ 43,179.01	$ 6,476.85	$ 647.69	$ 7,124.54
5	35	$ 50,513.33	$ 7,577.00	$ 4,251.59	$ 46,767.49
10	40	$ 61.457.19	$ 9,218.58	$ 12,019.94	$ 132,219.31
15	45	$ 74,772.07	$ 11,215.81	$ 25,651.62	$ 282,167.83
20	50	$ 90,971.66	$ 13,645.75	$ 48,969.06	$ 538,659.71
25	55	$ 110,680.94	$ 16,602.14	$ 88,180.93	$ 969,990.18
30	60	$ 134,660.28	$ 20,199.04	$ 153,350.31	$ 1,686,853.36
35	65	$ 163,834.82	$ 24,575.22	$ 260,761.80	$ 2,868,379.76
40	70	$ 199,330.11	$ 29,899.52	$ 436,736.63	$ 4,804,102.96
46	76	$ 252,216.18	$ 37,832.43	$ 799,942.00	**$ 8,799,361.96**

In 46 years, the value of this fifteen millions dollars is approximately equal to $1,731,425.00 in today's dollars (assuming 3% annual inflation).

... not as much, but still pretty good, don't you think? It proves that just because you're not in your early twenties, you can still amass wealth if you start saving now.

Finally, here is what you would be able to save if you waited until you were 46 – which is closer to when most people start thinking about serious saving:

Year	Age	Income	Deposit (15% of income)	Interest	Total Value of Investment
1	46	$ 77,762.96	$ 11,664.44	$ 1,166.44	$ 12,830.88
5	50	$ 90,971.66	$ 13,645.75	$ 7,656.87	$ 84,225.61
10	55	$ 110,680.94	$ 16,602.14	$ 21,647.23	$ 238,119.51
15	60	$ 134,660.29	$ 20,199.04	$ 46,197.12	$ 508,168.33
20	65	$ 163,834.83	$ 24,575.22	$ 88,190.52	$ 970,095.74
25	70	$ 199,330.12	$ 29,899.52	$ 158,808.87	$ 1,746,897.57
31	76	$ 252,216.19	$ 37,832.43	$ 307,576.01	**$ 3,383,336.14**

In 31 years, the value of this fifteen millions dollars is approximately equal to $655,729.00 in today's dollars (assuming 3% annual inflation).

If you were to live on 90% of your final annual income, this would be just under 3 years of living expenses. When starting your savings past 40, it's a good idea to have another retirement plan to supplement these savings, or perhaps a more aggressive plan than 15% of your income.

Credit & Credit Card Basics

Credit: Why it's good

Credit is a tool that allows you to buy something in payments – or finance something. Certain items are almost impossible to save for. For example, a house: most of us would find it difficult to save enough money to pay for a home – it might take 20 or 30 years to save enough!

Credit cards can be good. They allow you not to carry cash, and they let you order things over the phone or online. They're often needed for security deposits when you want to rent a car or reserve a hotel room, so they can be very handy. As long as you can pay for what you bought when the bill comes, credit cards are fine.

Flash Point!
Credit: When it's bad
Credit gets bad when you use it as a way to get things you can't afford. An example of this is having a credit card that is *"maxed out,"* or spent all the way to its limit, and never really gets paid off. When this happens, it means that – somewhere along the way – you bought things you couldn't really pay for.

Getting and establishing credit
Before any bank will give you a loan for something major like a house, they'll want to see your credit history. Every time you apply for or receive a loan, or a credit card - and sometimes even rent an apartment – a record will go on your permanent credit history. This credit history is attached to your name and social security number and follows you for life. Your credit history shows not only what credit you have received, but how much you owe at any given time, how promptly you make your payments, and details of any late and/or missed payments you made.

Credit cards: The easiest way to establish credit

How to get a credit card
Sometimes it can be hard to get your first credit card. Annoyingly, many companies won't give you credit until you can prove a credit history, and you can't prove a credit history until you can get credit! Start with your own bank, and check with your financial aid office at school; certain companies are more willing to give credit to students and they have usually sent brochures to college financial aid offices.

IMPORTANT: Are you the only one with a credit card?
Something about spending money on credit makes people spend a little more freely than they would if they were handing over the cash. This goes for your friends, too.

If six of you would like to go to a concert, and you're the only one with a credit card, it may seem logical that you would put the tickets on your card and let your friends pay you back. Same with a trip away for hotel rooms, train and plane tickets. However, if you do provide this service, it's fair to ask that they give you the money before you charge the items.

Sometimes, even with the best intentions, somebody won't be able to pay, and it's YOU that gets stuck with the bill, and put in the uncomfortable position of asking for your money.

Fees, and how credit cards work

Credit isn't a free service that's offered to good, upstanding citizens – it's big business, and a major money-maker for credit companies. How do they make their money?

~ By charging you an annual fee to have a card.
~ By charging interest on the purchases you make that aren't paid off at the end of the month.
~ By charging you cash-advance fees and extra interest.
~ By charging the retailer a percentage of the sale, as well as monthly fees and renting out the little terminals that process your card.

When it comes to making money, credit card companies have a lot of angles – and it's up to you to be familiar with the fine print, learn the details, and be a savvy credit consumer.

Interest

Here's the deal: Interest is charged on the balance remaining on your card that is not paid off by the due date. It is separate from the minimum payment, which is always due no matter what.

To illustrate, let's say you buy a new pair of jeans for $40. The bill comes, the balance is $40, and your due date is the 15th of the month. You decide to pay the minimum payment of $10 only. That means you will be charged interest on the remaining $30, and that interest will be added to your balance on your next statement. If you don't pay the balance off the next month, interest will be calculated on the remaining $30, plus the interest you were charged last month. Of course, interest will be charged on any new purchases not paid for, too.

Annual Fees

Many cards charge you an annual fee for having and using their card. Try shopping for a card that doesn't, or ask your bank to waive this fee based on other companies that don't charge it.

Grace Period

You'll see this term referred to a lot in the world of credit. It is the amount of time between when you charge an item, and the due date on your bill, which is also called a statement. Interest is not normally charged during this time, with the exception of cash advances.

What do we mean, *"with the exception of cash advances"*? Great question! When you have an available balance on your credit card (meaning you've got room to charge stuff) you almost always have the option of using the card like an ATM card and getting cash. The catch is that you are usually charged a fee, plus interest from the moment you take the cash. Sometimes, the interest rate is even higher than your agreed interest rate on the card … cha-ching!

Minimum Payments on credit cards

A minimum payment on a credit card is an amount, usually a percentage of the total amount you owe (called your balance), that you have to pay by the due date.

> **Here's an example:**
>
> You buy a new pair of jeans for $40. The bill comes, the balance is $40, and your due date is the 15th of next month. You'll see a line on your statement (a credit card bill showing all your purchases) that says something like *"Minimum payment due: $10.00."*
>
> This means that, by the 15th, you can make a payment of $10 or more - but no less.

Most cards have a minimum on their minimums, and it's usually around $10. So, even if your balance is $11, you will still have to pay a minimum of $10.

Minimum payments increase with your balance (the total amount due) so keep this in mind when budgeting. They're usually around 2% of your balance, but find out what your credit card company charges.

Know your limits

All credit cards have a limit. If your card has a limit of $500, it means you are breaking your agreement if you charge over $500. You will generally not be allowed to charge this much, and if you are, it could result in extra fees or penalty interest, and it's also a permanent bad mark on your credit history.

Lost or stolen cards

If your card is lost or stolen, report it ***immediately***. If you're not sure that it's lost – for example you can't find your wallet, but you don't know if it was stolen or you just lost it, it is better to report cards stolen – even if they do turn up later.

Most card agreements offer protection if charges are made while your card is stolen. This means if somebody steals your card and charges $600 worth of stuff at The Gap, you won't be liable for payment.

It's important to call and notify your card company as soon as you realize your card is gone, because there is a limit placed on how long you have to report a stolen card and still be protected. It can be as few as two days – if your card was stolen on a Friday and you didn't realize or report it until Monday, you could lose your protection and be responsible for paying for everything the thief bought! It's a good idea to write down the phone number the credit card company provides to report theft. It's often on the back of the card, but that doesn't do you much good if it's been stolen! You definitely don't want to add to your stress by not being able to report the incident.

Store Cards and other credit sources

Many department stores, major chain shops and catalog companies offer their own credit cards. Often they'll offer instant approval if you have a regular credit card. This works by a quick check of your credit and ... voila, you've got credit. They often sweeten the deal by offering you 10% off everything you buy that same day.

Flash Point!
It is almost NEVER worth accepting this credit. Having too many outstanding credit lines lowers your credit score. Stick to your major credit card, which will work in these stores as well as their own card. If you feel tempted, ask yourself, *"Am I looking for a way to buy things I can't afford?"* If the answer is no, then put it on your regular card or pay a visit to the ATM and buy it with cash.

If the answer is yes, walk away! For being strong enough to walk away, be sure and reward yourself with a low-or-no-cost treat. You deserve it!

Financial Aid

Getting to know your financial aid advisor

Being at college, you have the best source of financial aid information you could ever hope for: the office of student aid at your school. They work with financial aid every day of the week, and are there to help you, so get to know them! If you have questions, need help with something, or have a change of circumstances, make an appointment and ask the experts.

Here are some tips on how to help your financial aid advisor give you the best service possible:

Flash Point!
Be kind, and patient. Financial aid advisors deal with thousands of details every day, and sometimes feel like they're in a totally thankless job. Treating your advisor nicely will get you a lot further than being pushy.

~ Make sure you are organized, and bring the documentation required. When you call to schedule your appointment, find out what you need to bring. Make a list, and double check that you have everything before you leave for your appointment.

- Prepare yourself for lots of paperwork and bureaucracy. It's not fun, but your hard work and patience will pay off in the end.

Traveling and Money
When you travel outside the country, you'll need to learn to work with another currency. It's pretty easy to learn, since most countries have banking systems similar to ours.

The first step when you're heading abroad is to find out what the exchange rate is against the dollar. This simply lets you know how much of the foreign currency you can buy for a dollar– and helps when you're making your plans. To budget for your trip, you'll need to know what you'll really be spending.

For example, is a hostel that charges 1,117 Japanese Yen expensive, or cheap?

You'll find that some countries offer a better deal for your money than others. Even countries that share the same currency, as they do in Europe, can vary greatly in everyday costs.

So where can you find the information? Your local bank should be able to provide it, and your newspaper usually lists current exchange rates. There are some great resources online, too.

Rates change – so watch out!
Rates do change, and if you're traveling on a tight budget, you might want to keep an eye on these changes. A small rate change can make a big difference to your spending money while you're there.

How to get your money when you're away

ATMs
Most countries have plenty of ATMs available. You can easily use your ATM card or debit card at almost all of these. The great thing about gaining access to your money this way is not having to carry the whole of your spending money with you during your trip. You can simply take out what you need, and leave the rest safely in your account. Be aware that you will be charged a fee – usually a couple of bucks – each time you withdraw money. Check with your bank before you go to make sure the fee is not too high.

To avoid extra charges for using your card out of the country, steer clear of freestanding machines that you might find in shopping malls and stores. They sometimes add their own very high fee.

Another advantage to ATM cards is that you get a direct exchange rate from your bank, which is usually better than a bank abroad will offer you to exchange dollars, and MUCH better than a currency exchange center, such as you might find in an airport.

If you're traveling through several countries with different currencies, an ATM card prevents you from having to exchange money and think about different currencies each time.

Flash Point!
Some ATMs have the numbers arranged backwards – like a phone, and some arrange them from one to nine, starting at the top. If you remember your PIN by letters instead of numbers, be aware that many ATMs don't have the letters like they do at home, so just be sure you check the arrangement and make it match your code!

Credit Cards

Your credit card is another good tool for use abroad. You'll get the same preferred exchange rate. The downside is they are not always accepted, and your bank may charge a fee for use overseas. Check in advance with your bank to find out. You may also want to check with your bank before traveling to find out if you need pre-approval to use your card abroad. Sometimes, the fraud protection mechanisms lenders have in place will decline any charges that you try to make from a foreign country.

Traveler's Checks

Traveler's checks need to be bought before you leave, and can be used as cash in places that accept them. You can also cash them in most banks abroad, and use the cash wherever you want.

The downside to traveler's checks is that you won't be able to cash them on weekends and at night when banks are closed, and even when banks are open, you'll have to wait in line. Some hotels and department stores offer this service, but they give you a poor exchange rate for your money.

Currency Exchange Centers

You'll find these in every airport, and in many towns abroad. They will happily exchange your dollars for the local currency, but check the rates - they are not always the most competitive. In fact, the more convenient the location, the poorer the rate you can expect!

Money Safety

When you're away, pay a lot of attention to your surroundings, and avoid pulling out wads of cash. Everyone knows that someone traveling has a decent amount of money with them – especially thieves. Keep your money as close to your body as you can – you can even buy little pouches that hang around your neck or buckle around your waist. It's safest to keep just a little bit of spending money in your pocket or wallet, and most of it in the pouch with your passport, credit cards and bank cards.

If you're carrying a backpack or handbag, avoid putting your wallet in an outside pocket that can be accessed easily by someone wanting to rip you off.

Help!

If you're ever in need of serious help while in another country, including losing or having your passport stolen, contact the American Embassy, or the Embassy of the country that issued your passport. They are there to help you with every imaginable sort of problem that could come up, and they do a great job.

The Moral of the Story

Be savvy when it comes to money. Shop around, save where you can, and don't spend more than you can afford. No one has an infinite amount of money so whether you choose to recognize it or not, you have a budget. Choosing not to acknowledge this causes a lot of stress; sometimes quickly, but always in the long run. You have enough to think about and worry about in college without adding money problems to the pile.

Taking a few moments to get a handle on your finances now can help make your life run more smoothly. When you keep an eye on your money and spend only what you plan to spend, you can relax, knowing you have enough to pay for everything that can come up.

Now that we've covered most of the money situations you might face in college, why not take the Financial Awareness quiz again and see if you've improved your score?

~ Chapter Ten ~
Knights in Shining Armor: Getting Help

Being in college - especially if you are living away from home for the first time - can be a trying experience. It has taken the whole of this book and an arsenal of online assessments and activities to help you plan for the challenges you might face. But what do you do if everything doesn't go according to plan? What about when it all seems to go wrong, and you need assistance?

Don't be afraid to ask for help when you need it! Family, friends, counselors and instructors can point you in a direction for help, and they're usually happy that you've asked.

We've given you as much information as we could in this book, and the more you take the time to complete the assessments, think about our exercises and journal, or talk about your thoughts, the better chance you have of things going well in college.

As for some unfortunate unforeseen events, remember to have confidence in your ability to work things through. Think positively, even when things seem impossible, and take action when you feel the time is right, even if it feels easier to stay stuck.

To end this book, we've created a reference of resources on the following pages for every sort of problem to assist you in finding help. Think of it as a troubleshooting guide to college life. It's one final way for us to help you achieve college success. Get to know yourself, work hard, and good luck!

Flash Point!
If you don't find what you are looking for here, please use our resource finder tool online. There are hundreds of really useful contacts in our database.

Resources

Academic Issues

Source of Help	Back to College
Contact	*www.back2college.com/library/gettingstarted.htm*

Alcohol

Source of Help	Alcoholics Anonymous
Contact	*www.alcoholics-anonymous.org*

Depression

Source of Help	Depression.com
Contact	*www.depression.com*

Discrimination

Source of Help	NAACP *or* EEOC
Contact	*www.naacp.org or www.eeoc.gov*

Domestic Violence

Source of Help	Domestic Violence Hotline
Contact	*www.ndvh.org*

Drugs

Source of Help	Center for Substance Abuse Hotline
Contact	800.662.4357

Eating Disorders

Source of Help	National Eating Disorders Association
Contact	www.edap.org/p.asp?WebPage_ID=331

Finance (credit card debt)

Source of Help	Practical Money Skills for Life
Contact	*www.practicalmoneyskills.com/english/at_home/consumers/credit*

Resources

Finance (general)

Source of Help	Young Money
Contact	*www.youngmoney.com/money_management*

Grief Support

Source of Help	GriefNet
Contact	*www.griefnet.org*

Homesickness

Source of Help	10 Helpful Hints for Overcoming Homesickness
Contact	*idid.essortment.com/collegestudent_phu.htm*

Obesity

Source of Help	American Obesity Association
Contact	*www.obesity.org*

Pregnancy

Source of Help	Healthline
Contact	*www.healthline.com/channel/pregnancy.html*

Rape

Source of Help	Rape, Abuse and Incest National Network
Contact	*www.rainn.org*

Roommate Issues

Source of Help	Chapter Eight: Kissing Frogs: Getting Along Using the PLSI
Contact	Both of you should take the PLSI online!

Self-injury

Source of Help	S.A.F.E Alternatives
Contact	*www.selfinjury.com*

Resources

Sexual Health

Source of Help	SexualHealth.com
Contact	*www.sexualhealth.com*

Smoking

Source of Help	Centers for Disease Control and Prevention
Contact	*www.cdc.gov/tobacco*

Stalking

Source of Help	StalkingVictims.com
Contact	*www.stalkingvictims.com*

Suicide

Source of Help	American Foundation for Suicide Prevention
Contact	*www.afsp.org*

Theft (general)

Source of Help	Campus Security or 911
Contact	911

Theft (identity)

Source of Help	Federal Trade Commission - Identity Theft
Contact	*www.ftc.gov/bcp/edu/microsites/idtheft*

Flash Point!
If you find something really useful, you can add it to the blank resource spaces on the following pages. These spaces are also great places to write down important contacts at your school.

My Resources

Important Resource

Source of Help ____________________

Contact ____________________

Important Resource

Source of Help ____________________

Contact ____________________

Important Resource

Source of Help ____________________

Contact ____________________

Important Resource

Source of Help ____________________

Contact ____________________

Important Resource

Source of Help ____________________

Contact ____________________

Important Resource

Source of Help ____________________

Contact ____________________

Important Resource

Source of Help ____________________

Contact ____________________

Important Resource

Source of Help ____________________

Contact ____________________

My Resources

Important Resource ______________________
Source of Help ______________________
Contact ______________________

Important Resource ______________________
Source of Help ______________________
Contact ______________________

Important Resource ______________________
Source of Help ______________________
Contact ______________________

Important Resource ______________________
Source of Help ______________________
Contact ______________________

Important Resource ______________________
Source of Help ______________________
Contact ______________________

Important Resource ______________________
Source of Help ______________________
Contact ______________________

Important Resource ______________________
Source of Help ______________________
Contact ______________________

Important Resource ______________________
Source of Help ______________________
Contact ______________________

My Profile

For more information on Sensory Learning Styles see: *Chapter Six: Excelling in the Classroom Without Being Grumpy, Sleepy or Dopey.*
For more information on the DISC Assessment see: *Chapter Seven: Mirror, Mirror: the DISC Assessment.*
For more information on the PLSI Assessment see: *Chapter Eight: Getting Along Using the PLSI.*

My Sensory Learning Style

My Sensory Learning Style

My PLSI Assessment

My PLSI Assessment

My DISC Assessment

My DISC Assessment

My Mission Statement

For more information on Mission Statements see: *page 46 or online under the Tools menu.*

My Tagline

For more information on Taglines see: *page 80.*

My Notes

Make this book about you!

We've made a big deal about doing things your way. So, we left some space here for you to make notes about anything you want. As you're reading or working online, use the following blank pages to jot down page numbers, web site addresses, quotes, flash points, or even phone numbers, or new ideas. For big concepts you want to revisit, this is a great place to write a few words to jog your memory later. Remember that the act of writing really helps you retain information.

My Notes

My Notes

~ About the Authors ~

Sidney Pogatchnik

Sidney Pogatchnik

Sidney Pogatchnik is a professional writer whose specialty is making complex concepts easy to understand. Previous works have included topics such as *Personality and Temperament, Communication Skills, Finance* and *Motivational writing.* A native of California, Sidney has worked throughout the world and currently resides in Ireland.

Sidney's DISC and PLSI assessments

•**DISC:** ISdc	***PLSI:** ENTP

Mark Kroh

Mark Kroh

Mark Kroh, CEO of Campus ToolKit, left his position as the Campus Director of an Art and Design college to create an interactive system that *helps students build* the *foundation skills* they need *to succeed in school.* Mark's background in higher education, technology and design have led to a unique system that tailors students' experiences to their own individual needs.

Mark's DISC and PLSI assessments

•**DISC:** CDSi	***PLSI:** INTJ

• For more information on the DISC Assessment see:
Chapter Seven: Mirror, Mirror: the DISC Assessment

* For more information on the PLSI Assessment see:
Chapter Eight: Getting Along Using the PLSI